Travelog

Edition 2

Published by Druk Asia Publishing
©Druk Asia 2025
ISBN 978-981-18-8724-6

First Edition (September 2021)
Second Edition (March 2023)
Second Edition (Updated November 2025)

Visit **www.bhutantravelog.com** for updates and digital content.

To reach out to the publisher, email **hello@bhutantravelog.com**.

The resources in this book have been provided for informational purposes only. Although the authors have made every effort and taken reasonable care in preparing the book, we cannot warrant the accuracy, adequacy or completeness of the content, and disclaim all liability arising from the use of any of the information.

Front cover image by Michael Lee
Book design by Steve Lim Seng Hee
Edited by Lee Chow Ping
Illustrations by Defry
Photography by Andrew Chun, Ashley Chen, Bhupen Ghimiray, Derek Low, Dorji Dradhul, Inez Bratahalim, Joni Herison, Karma Dorji, Kencho Wangdi, Lester V. Ledesma, Michael Lee, Sathya Parthasarathi, Scott A. Woodward, Stephen Gollan, Tian Chad, Tom White, Ugyen Dema, Wiris William, Yeshey Dorji, Zahariz Khuzaimah, Bumdeling Wildlife Sanctuary, Royal Office for Media and Department of Tourism.

Acknowledgements

We want to express our sincere thanks to the numerous people who played a crucial role in bringing this book to fruition. Most notably, we would like to convey our profound appreciation to the esteemed former Prime Minister of Bhutan, Dasho Dr. Lotay Tshering, for generously dedicating his time to write the foreword and share his insights.

Special appreciation goes out to those who graciously shared their photographs and personal experiences in Bhutan, including Dino & Vanita, James Low, Linda Leaming, Walter Escaño, Françoise Pommaret, Kristine Li, and Bradley Mayhew.

We extend our profound gratitude to the talented photographers who accompanied us on this journey and contributed their stunning photographs to the book, including Michael Lee, Andrew Chun, Bhupen Ghimiray, Derek Low, Dorji Dhradhul, Inez Bratahalim, Karma Dorji, Kencho Wangdi, Lester V. Ledesma, Sathya Parthasarathi, Scott A. Woodward, Stephen Gollan, Tian Chad, Tom White, Ugyen Dema, Wiris William, Yeshey Dorji, and Zahariz Khuzaimah.

We are very grateful to our illustrator, Defry, for all the lovely illustrations. Thank you very much to our editor, Chow Ping, for her insightful feedback, comments and suggestions. Our utmost gratitude to our designer, Steve Lim, for his hard work and dedication throughout the creative process.

We greatly appreciate Dasho Kinley Dorji and Pek Sioksian for helping us to proofread and edit parts of the book. Their experience and valuable insights have been extremely enriching for us.

We would also like to thank all our friends in Bhutan including Damcho Rinzin and the Department of Tourism who have provided support and encouragement throughout the years. Your friendship and generosity propelled us to continue sharing the beauty of the kingdom with the world.

Last but not least, thank you for picking up this book and supporting our humble efforts in showing you a glimpse of this enchanting country called Bhutan, a special place that is very close to our hearts.

It is always a pleasure to be a part of the publication that my friend Ashley Chen passionately puts together. More so, it is dedicated to Bhutan, a country that is so apart in values and experiences that I take so much pride in sharing.

The last time I contributed to the earlier edition of the travelogue, I was in a quarantine facility, during the peak of the pandemic. I was returning from an official trip abroad and was fulfilling the mandatory 21-day quarantine requirement. Looking back, so much changed since then.

Bhutan is today applauded for our successful management of the pandemic. It did not come easy. It entailed so much effort and sacrifices. In the same spirit, my country chose to embark on a journey to reset ourselves and our priorities soon after the pandemic.

As I write this, Bhutan is living an unprecedented change. The national transformation and systemic reforms are underway in size and manner never seen before. We are at a critical crossroad, as we strive to attain high-income status as soon as possible. For information, Bhutan has graduated from the Least Developed Country status in December 2023.

Which is why we have to get the tourism sector right. I believe that tourism is like a mirror that reflects the significant qualities of a nation. If we are to be a progressive country with all our values and priorities in the right place, we have to relook at the tourism sector from a crystalline lens.

It has to be beyond the pristine landscapes and colourful festivals we offer. It has to be above our commitment to sustainability, and cultural and environmental preservation. Reinforcing our guiding philosophy of Gross National Happiness, it has to be about the ultimate expression of our existence and celebration of life.

Which is why the brand "Bhutan Believe". It is about believing in ourselves, in our modest efforts and in cherishing what we have, while seeking to transform. To achieve anything meaningful in life, we must believe.

And thus, on this extraordinary journey of ours, we urge everyone to be a part of it. As you delve into the pages of this publication and subsequently into the folds of our mountains and valleys, may you discover the treasure that leaves an indelible mark on your soul.

Dasho Dr Lotay Tshering
Former Prime Minister
Royal Government of Bhutan

Which is why the brand "Bhutan Believe". It is about believing in ourselves, in our modest efforts and in cherishing what we have, while seeking to transform. To achieve anything meaningful in life, we must believe.

Bhutan Believe

It has been five years since the COVID-19 pandemic initially brought global tourism to a standstill. In this span of time, numerous developments and shifts have occurred within our personal lives, the environment, and our country. The unprecedented pandemic has left an indelible mark, and Bhutan is no exception to these changes.

During this period, Bhutan, often referred to as the "Land of the Thunder Dragon," has undertaken several adjustments to its tourism policy. These adaptations are being made in order to effectively tackle the ongoing challenges and uncertainties of the future. Bhutan's position is truly unique, and it faces its own set of challenges and circumstances that set it apart from other nations. This phase of change signifies both the resilience and adaptability of the country as it endeavors to shape a future that aligns with its distinct identity and values.

In September 2022, a significant development unfolded as the Department of Tourism unveiled the fresh and revitalizing tagline for Brand Bhutan: "Bhutan Believe." This new tagline symbolises a transformative journey and embodies an unwavering spirit of hope and positivity, intended to kindle feelings of pride and ignite the creative minds of both the nation's citizens and its visitors.

For the Bhutanese, "Bhutan Believe" holds a deeply personal significance. It encapsulates the essence of self-belief and faith in the future. It encourages a collective sense of confidence and conviction in realising the country's aspirations.

To those who hold a fascination for Bhutan, "Bhutan Believe" conveys a powerful message. It urges us to embrace a belief in the endeavors that Bhutan is striving to accomplish.

Bhutan Travelog Edition 2 aims to provide you with insights into the country's history, values, customs, as well as travel tips and recommendations. This book also includes 8 exclusive first-hand stories from diverse travellers who have been to Bhutan to provide you with a glimpse into this idyllic country. We hope that their journeys will spark your curiosity and inspire your own journey to this breathtaking kingdom.

Special Feature

Michael Lee is a travel entrepreneur and a qualified UK Master Photographer (UKMPA). He has been extensively traveling off the beaten path in Asia and Africa for almost 20 years.

Michael conducts regular photography workshops at Leica Akademie, specializing in street candid, cultural, and landscape photography, as well as travel photography. His deep respect for people and cultures inspires new ideas in his workshops and tours, allowing him to capture the essence of the journey in its purest form.

Keep a lookout for these icons!

The icons are here to help you navigate your reading.

Tips

Tips are important information for tourists who are new to Bhutan. These are things that you should take note of when you're planning a trip to Bhutan.

Ancient Fortresses

This icon represents the great majestic *dzong* (ancient fortresses) of Bhutan. Each district has at least one dzong that serves as the district monastic body and government administrative centre.

General Sightseeing

These places are for general sightseeing. It's where you get your camera ready for action. Even if you are not a shutterbug, you can simply relax and drink in the stunning landscapes and architecture of the sites.

Activities (Booking required)

If you come across a calendar icon, note that there are activities available on-site. Prior booking is often required. Discuss with your tour operator to make arrangements in advance.

Religious Sites

When you see the stupa icon, it means that the place is a sacred site. It can either be a nunnery, a temple, or a place with great religious significance.

Myths and Legends

Bhutan is a country steeped in mythology and folktales. The mystical dragon icon means that the particular site has intriguing myths or legends associated with it. Be sure to delve deeper into it with your tour guide when you are in Bhutan.

Bridges

Due to the mountainous terrains, Bhutanese rely on either suspension bridges or traditional cantilever bridges to get across the crystal-clear rivers. In fact, suspension bridges in Europe were influenced by the iron chain bridges in Bhutan, built by Thangthong Gyalpo.

Festivals

Festivals are very significant in Bhutanese culture. The dancer icon means that the site is a venue for certain festivals in Bhutan. However, the festival dates vary from year to year. For updated information on festival dates, check out **www.bhutantravelog.com.**

Arts and Crafts

There are 13 traditional *zorig chusum* (arts and crafts) in Bhutan, categorised during the reign of the fourth secular ruler, Tenzin Rabgye. These arts and crafts are integral to Bhutanese culture. The flower icon indicates that the location is popular for Bhutanese traditional arts and crafts.

Proverbs

Bhutanese are generally witty and you're bound to find nuggets of wisdom from the locals that you interact with. Their sense of humour is evident from their fun road signs. Thus, to spice up your reading, we have also inserted some interesting Bhutanese proverbs through the pages.

Proverb

འཇིག་རྟེན་མ་ཕྱིས་དམ་ཆོས་མ་ཧ།

Jig ten ma chi; dam choe ma ha.

Do not start your worldly life too late; do not start your religious life too early.

Contents

About Bhutan

The first part of the book features the important symbols, history, and governance system of Bhutan. It serves as a glimpse into the kingdom and provides basic understanding of the foundation on which the nation has been built upon.

Map of Bhutan

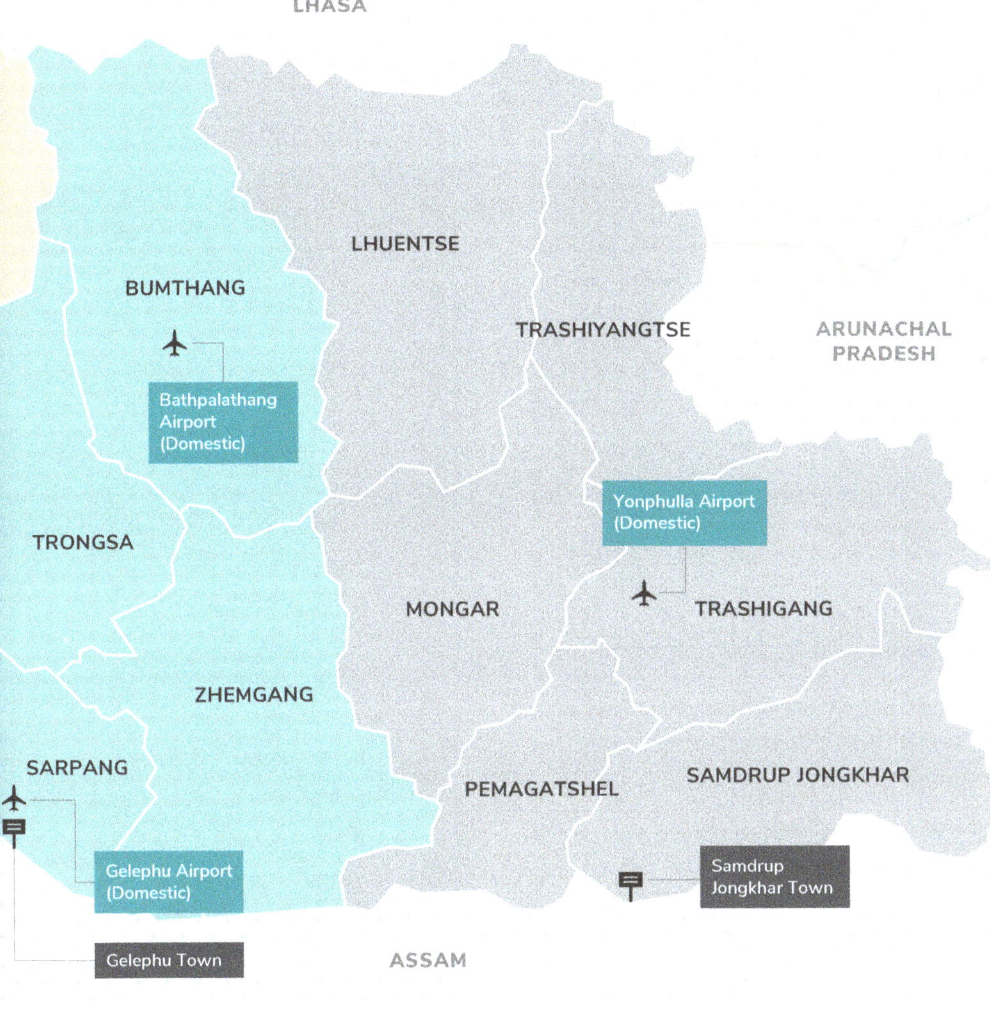

Bhutan is divided into 20 districts (dzongkhag) and 3 regions.
West
Central
East
Capital of Bhutan
Airports
Border Checkpoints
Tibet (Autonomous Region of China)
LHASA
BUMTHANG
LHUENTSE
TRASHIYANGTSE
ARUNACHAL PRADESH
Bathpalathang Airport (Domestic)
Yonphulla Airport (Domestic)
TRONGSA
MONGAR
TRASHIGANG
ZHEMGANG
SARPANG
PEMAGATSHEL
SAMDRUP JONGKHAR
Gelephu Airport (Domestic)
Samdrup Jongkhar Town
Gelephu Town
ASSAM
India

Bhutan is also known as **Druk Yul** — Land of Thunder Dragon.

Bhutan, officially known as the **Kingdom of Bhutan**, is a landlocked country in South Asia. The kingdom is sandwiched between two giant countries — China in the north and India in the south. Located in the Eastern Himalayas, Bhutan is bordered by the Tibet Autonomous Region of China in the north, Sikkim (India) and Chumbi Valley (Tibet) in the west, Arunachal Pradesh (India) in the east, as well as Assam (India) and West Bengal (India) in the south.

Bhutan has a total land area of around 38,400 km² with elevations ranging from 300 m in the southern foothills to 7,000 m in the north.

The country is surrounded by the Himalayas in the north and west. The highest point in Bhutan is Gangkhar Puensum, which has the distinction of being the highest unclimbed mountain in the world, at 7,570 m.

The word *druk* or 'thunder dragon' first originated in Tibet. Legend has it that Tsangpa Gyarey, a renowned meditation master and ancestor of Bhutan's founding father, Zhabdrung Ngawang Namgyal, was visiting Nam Village in Lhasa, Tibet to set up a spiritual centre.

On his visit there, he was reported to have seen nine dragons flying, triggering a clap of booming thunder in the sky as he approached them. Reading all these as auspicious omens, he named the centre Druk, and his spiritual tradition took the derivative name Drukpa.

Local historians claim that Bhutan was called Drukyul and her people Drukpa after most people converted to the Drukpa school of Buddhism. Before becoming Druk Yul, Bhutan was known as Lho Jong 'The Valleys of the South' or Lho Jong Menjong 'The Southern Valleys of Medicinal Herbs'.

Bhutan is also known to be one of the world's last surviving Buddhist kingdom. And some say, the last Shangri-La.

The Kingdom of Bhutan made international headlines when it became a democratic, constitutional monarchy in 2008.

Majestic Gangkhar Phuensum with its towering peaks

National Symbols

National Flag

Bhutan's national flag is divided diagonally into two halves of yellow and orange. The upper half in yellow symbolises the king as the upholder of the spiritual and secular foundations of Bhutan. The lower orange symbolises the flourishing of Buddhist teachings, manifested in the Drukpa Kagyu and Nyingmapa traditions. The dragon signifies the name and purity of the country: Druk Yul, Land of Thunder Dragon, while the jewels in its claws denote the country's wealth and perfection.

National Emblem

The national emblem of Bhutan maintains some of the emblems of the national flag. It is contained in a circle with a crossed *dorje* (thunderbolts) in the centre, placed above a lotus and flanked by two thunder dragons. In the compassionate form of Triple Gem, the sacred jewel at the top of the royal crest symbolises the supremacy of the sovereign in the Buddhist Kingdom of Bhutan while the lotus represents purity.

The crossed dorjes placed above the lotus represent the harmonious relationship between the traditional customs of spiritual law and modern authority. The male and female thunder dragons with snarling mouths symbolise the country's guardian deities protecting the country.

Climate

Bhutan has a variety of climates due to varying altitudes and terrain. The south has a hot and humid subtropical climate, and the southern foothills experience the heaviest rainfall due to the southwest monsoon flowing from the Bay of Bengal. The west-central part has temperate climates with warm summers, and cool winters with snowfall occurring occasionally. In the northern region, the weather is much colder during winter. Mountain peaks are perpetually covered in snow, while lower parts are still cool during summer due to the high altitude.

Seasons

Bhutan has four distinct seasons. Spring in Bhutan is relatively short. It usually starts in early March and lasts until mid-April. Summer with occasional showers happens from mid-April until late June, whereas heavier summer rain lasts from late June until late September. Autumn follows until late November, and winter sets in from then until March.

Population

Bhutan has a population of approximately 798,000 people (as of 2025), which is equivalent to 0.01% of the total world population. The population density in Bhutan is 20 people per km². Nearly half, or 45.8% of the population lives in urban areas.

The Bhutanese

Ngalop, Sharchokpa and Lhotshampa

There are three major ethnic groups in Bhutan:
Ngalop, Sharchokpa and Lhotshampa. They are
also collectively known as Drukpas (literally,
people from Bhutan).

Aside from the three major ethnic groups,
Bhutan has nomadic communities living in the
highlands such as the Brokpas in the east, and
the Layaps and Lunaps in the northern part of
Bhutan.

National Language

Dzongkha

The national language of Bhutan is Dzongkha.
There are two other major languages,
Tshanglakha and Lotshamkha. In total, there
are 19 different languages and dialects spoken
throughout the country.

Spiritual Practices

Buddhism

Bhutanese predominantly practice
Vajrayana Buddhism (Drukpa Kagyu and
Nyingmapa traditions).

National Animal

Takin

Bhutan's national animal is the takin (*Budorcas taxicolor*), a rare mammal that is often associated with religious history and mythology. There is a takin preserve in Motithang in Thimphu, where tourists can visit to catch a glimpse of this unique national animal.

National Flower

Himalayan Blue Poppy

The national flower of Bhutan is the Himalayan blue poppy (*Meconopsis gakyidiana*). It is a rare flower that grows at an elevation of 3,700 - 4,300 metres above sea level. The elusive Himalayan blue poppies can be found in eastern Bhutan, particularly in Merak and Sakteng.

National Tree

Himalayan Cypress

The national tree of Bhutan is the Himalayan cypress (*Cupressus torulosa*). Cypresses are found in abundance and easily noticeable near temples and monasteries. The cypresses grow in temperate climate zones between 1,800 - 3,500 metres.

National Bird

Raven

The national bird of Bhutan is the raven. It represents one of the most powerful deities of the country, Jarog Dongchen.

The Royal Raven Crown worn by the kings of Bhutan represents the deep reverence that Bhutanese hold for these national birds as protective deities.

National Sport

Archery

Archery was declared the national sport in 1971 when Bhutan became a member of the United Nations. Bhutan also maintains an Olympics archery team.

Bhutanese regularly hold archery competitions and tournaments throughout the country. The target distance for archery in Bhutan is 145 metre, double that of an Olympics archery range.

National Butterfly

Ludlow's Bhutan Swallowtail

Ludlow's Bhutan swallowtail was originally discovered by botanists Frank Ludlow and George Sheriff in Bhutan around 1933-1934. It was rediscovered 75 years later by Karma Wangdi, a forestry officer, in August 2009. He collected the first evidence — a specimen of the butterfly — in Bumdeling Wildlife Sanctuary and proved that this rare butterfly can still be found in Bhutan. Ludlow's Bhutan swallowtail (*Bhutanitis ludlow*) was officially endorsed as the national butterfly in 2012.

History of Bhutan

Early History

Bhutan's vibrant history is strongly tied to Buddhism. You'll discover important spiritual masters of the Himalayas who played vital roles in Bhutan's early history. When trying to understand Bhutan's history, you have to open up your mind. Instead of rationalising the events, we suggest you visualise the essence of its spirituality. Absorb the interesting folklores about the kingdom.

Buddhism was first introduced to Bhutan in the 7th century when the Tibetan King, Songtsen Gampo, built Kyichu Lhakhang in Paro and Jambay Lhakhang in Bumthang — two of the 108 temples built to pin down a demoness.

It is believed that the demoness was obstructing the spread of Buddhism, and these two temples pinned down the left foot and left knee of the demoness who was subdued.

The Zhabdrung and the Dual System of Government, 1600 - 1907

Under the politically and religiously charismatic Ngawang Namgyal, Bhutan became a unified polity in the 17th century. Ngawang Namgyal was a religious master of the Drukpa school who held the honorary title of Zhabdrung Rinpoche, 'Precious Jewel at Whose Feet One Prostrates'. Persecuted in Tibet, he fled to Bhutan in 1616. Over the next 30 years, he unified the 'southern valleys' into the nation State of Druk Yul.

Zhabdrung Ngawang Namgyal provided Bhutan with a unique system of administration and law. He established the unique system of government with the Central Monastic Body under a religious leader, the Je Khenpo (chief abbot), and a political system administered by a temporal chief, the desi (secular ruler). This dual system of government, choesi, lasted until the Wangchuck dynasty took over in 1907.

You may see children as young as seven years old enrolled in a monastic school

Painting of Zhabdrung Ngawang Namgyal

Bhutan and the British

The 200 years prior to the establishment of the monarchy was the most unstable period in the history of Bhutan, with internal strife, civil wars and political turmoil. 22 desis were reported to be assassinated or deposed by rivals during these years, except for the 13th desi, Sheru Wangchuk, who ruled for 20 years. Between 1651 and 1730, Tibet invaded Bhutan around seven times. The political instability caused rival factions to seek support from the Chinese emperor in Beijing.

In 1730, the 10th desi, Mipham Wangmo, assisted Gya Chila, the ruler of Cooch Behar (present-day West Bengal), against intrusion in a family feud, thus allowing Bhutan to station a force in Cooch Behar. In 1768, the desi formed alliances with the Panchen Lama in Tibet and King Prithvi Narayan Shah of Nepal.

In 1772, Bhutan invaded Cooch Behar to help settle a feud over succession, resulting in Cooch Behar seeking assistance from the British East India Company. British East India Company drove the Bhutanese garrison out of Cooch Behar and later attacked Bhutan itself in 1773. The Druk Desi signed a Treaty of Peace with the British East India Company on April 25, 1774, where Bhutan agreed to return to its pre-1730 boundaries.

The Duar War

However, skirmishes over boundaries and trading rights continued with the British for the next 100 years. The continual skirmishes at the southern border escalated and eventually led to the Duar War (1864-1865), a confrontation over who would control the Bengal Duars. Bengal Duars is the area of plains between the Brahmaputra River up to the lowest hills of Bhutan.

The Duar War lasted only five months. It ended in Bhutan's defeat and loss of the Assam Duars and Bengal Duars. On November 11, 1865, Bhutan signed the Treaty of Sinchula to restore friendly relations and gave up the territories in exchange for an annuity from the British.

During this period, there was a civil war in Bhutan due to power struggles between the Paro and Trongsa valleys. The Trongsa's penlop (governor), Jigme Namgyal, eventually controlled central and eastern Bhutan. After his death, he was succeeded by his son, Ugyen Wangchuck, who defeated his political rivals in several civil wars, and was elected as the first hereditary King of Bhutan, marking the beginning of the Wangchuck dynasty.

Monarchy and Governance

In 2008, Bhutan became a constitutional monarchy, with His Majesty the fifth King as the Head of State. The kings of Bhutan are known as Druk Gyalpo, 'Dragon King'. Through the admirable stewardship of the Druk Gyalpos, Bhutan has shown excellent leadership in environmental preservation and balanced governance. They have maintained significant forest cover, provided a safe habitat for endangered species, and adopted many environmentally friendly and sustainable policies.

Ugyen Wangchuck

FIRST KING (1862 - 1926)

Ugyen Wangchuck was unanimously elected as the hereditary ruler of Bhutan by Bhutan's chiefs and principal lamas on December 17, 1907. He was crowned the Head of State and given the title Druk Gyalpo, ending the choesi, dual system of government.

The first King had developed close relations with the British by assisting in negotiations between Britain and Tibet. He was deeply aware that Bhutan would need support through times of regional conflict and rivalries.

During his reign, Bhutan remained largely isolated from the rest of the world.

Ugyen Wangchuck died in 1926 and was succeeded by his son, Jigme Wangchuck.

Jigme Wangchuck

SECOND KING (1905 - 1952)

Jigme Wangchuck became the second King of Bhutan in 1926 after the death of his father.

Jigme Wangchuck's reign saw significant administrative reforms in the country. He enforced a hierarchical system where the king had absolute power over all religious and secular matters. He also appointed a chief abbot to set up a central religious administrative body.

He is often credited for bringing modern education to Bhutan. In 1949, he signed the Indo-Bhutan Treaty with India, calling for peace between the two nations and reinforcing Bhutan's sovereignty and independence. He also continued his father's legacy by maintaining the country's isolation and ensuring political stability.

Jigme Dorji Wangchuck

THIRD KING (1929 - 1972)

Jigme Dorji Wangchuck, also fondly known as the Father of Modern Bhutan, succeeded the throne in 1952 following his father's death. He opened up Bhutan to the outside world, embarked on modernisation and kickstarted Bhutan's journey towards democracy. His education in England and exposure to many foreign countries provided him with broader political and economic perspectives. In 1953, he introduced democratic institutions in Bhutan including the *Tshogdu* (National Assembly), which had the power to remove the king or his successors with a two-thirds majority.

He formulated a new legal and judicial system and drafted the country's first economic development plan. He also developed Bhutan's infrastructure, including the transportation, education, communications, agriculture, and healthcare systems.

Jigme Dorji Wangchuck was the driving force behind the modern education system in Bhutan. More notably, Bhutan's isolation from the world ended under his reign. He viewed diplomatic relationships with other countries as integral to Bhutan's sovereignty and independence.

He died from a heart ailment on July 21, 1972, in Nairobi, Kenya, at the age of 43.

Jigme Singye Wangchuck

FOURTH KING (1955 - PRESENT, abdicated in 2006)

Jigme Singye Wangchuck assumed power in 1972 at the tender age of 17 following the sudden death of his father. Despite his youthfulness and lack of experience, he brought profound wisdom to the throne. He focused on economic self-reliance while preserving the culture, tradition, and natural environment of Bhutan. He also coined the renowned 'Gross National Happiness' philosophy to measure society's progress and development instead of Gross National Product. Bhutan's economy accelerated under his reign, during which he established industries in raw materials, agriculture and hydropower.

The King also focused on preserving and promoting national identity as part of the sixth Five-Year Plan introduced in 1987. He recognised that a solid distinct national identity was crucial for Bhutan's well-being and security. As part of the 'One Nation, One People' policy, the King issued a royal decree to strengthen the Bhutanese identity by promoting the Bhutanese etiquette, national dress and national language.

The far-sighted king also promulgated the 'High value, Low volume' tourism policy in the 1970s. This policy led to the strategy of avoiding mass tourism in Bhutan, to ensure economic returns while preserving the culture and environment.

Jigme Khesar Namgyel Wangchuck

FIFTH KING (1980 - PRESENT)

Jigme Khesar Namgyel Wangchuck ascended the throne on November 6, 2008. He was educated in India and the United States before attending Oxford University, where he studied politics and international relations. After his coronation, he launched the National Cadastral Resurvey, which focuses on improving the lives of Bhutanese living in remote areas.

He signed a new Treaty of Friendship with India in February 2007, replacing a 1949 treaty. He has launched numerous projects to inspire the elected government to address critical issues in governance, education, the rule of law, media, sustainable economic development, and preservation of the country's environmental and cultural heritage.

Jigme Khesar personally oversaw the peaceful transition from an absolute monarchy into a vibrant constitutional monarchy, just like his father had envisioned. The fifth King is popular and well-loved at home and abroad.

Along with Queen Jetsun Pema, the King travels internationally, raising the profile of Bhutan as a sovereign country. His humble and down-to-earth personality has earned him the title of 'People's King'.

In 2011, the King launched *Desuung* 'Guardians of Peace', a voluntary programme to encourage citizens to play an active role in nation-building by equipping them with skills and knowledge of disaster management. It's one of the most successful initiatives in the kingdom, and more than 22,000 volunteers have been trained under the programme.

During the 112th National Day address in 2019, the King announced that in 2022, Bhutan would kickstart *Gyalsung* (national service) for all Bhutanese who have reached the age of 18. Unlike national service in other countries that are mainly military-focused, the national service in Bhutan focuses on developing the skills and knowledge of the youths.

In 2020, during the coronavirus outbreak that affected the world, the King was at the forefront of the COVID-19 pandemic response in Bhutan. He provided extraordinary leadership and support to keep the people safe from the COVID-19 virus. Taking personal risks, he often toured the country to inspect preparations at vital locations. Upon his command, the Druk Gyalpo's Relief Kidu was set up to grant financial support to assist Bhutanese affected by the pandemic.

Throughout my reign, I will never rule you as a king. I will protect you as a parent, care for you as a brother and serve you as a son. I shall give you everything and keep nothing; I shall live such a life as a good human being that you may find it worthy to serve as an example for your children; I have no personal goals other than to fulfill your hopes and aspirations. I shall always serve, day and night, in the spirit of kindness, justice and equality.

Royal Family of Bhutan

King Jigme Khesar Namgyel Wangchuck, the Fifth Dragon King of Bhutan, married Jetsun Pema, the daughter of an airline pilot, in October 2011.

The King had announced his intent to marry earlier that year, and lovingly introduced his future bride to the people of Bhutan as someone who is "warm and kind in heart and character".

The royal couple has been blessed with two charming princes and an adorable newborn princess. The elder son, Gyalsey Jigme Namgyel Wangchuck, born in 2016, is the official heir to the throne. Their second son, Gyalsey Jigme Ugyen Wangchuck, born in 2020, adds to the family's joy and lineage. The third child, and first royal princess, Gyalsem Sonam Yangden Wangchuck was born on 9th September 2023.

The Bhutanese Royal Family serves as a symbol of optimism and a source of unity. They bring people together under a shared aspiration, standing as a beacon of hope that illuminates the kingdom.

Queen Jetsun Pema

On 13 October, 2011, Jetsun Pema was officially crowned the Queen of Bhutan at the age of 21 upon marrying King Jigme Khesar Namgyel Wangchuck. The world's youngest queen has often been praised for her beauty, kindness, intelligence and elegance. The beautiful Queen is an inspiration to all the women in Bhutan and beyond.

Find out more about Queen Jetsun Pema

s.bn.sg/jetsunpema

You can find portraits of the King and the royal family inside all the Bhutanese homes

Constitutional Monarchy

The modern political history of Bhutan is unique. Unlike many other countries where democracy was pursued by popular movements or civil wars, democracy in Bhutan was bestowed from the throne; Jigme Singye Wangchuck initiated the transition from absolute monarchy to constitutional monarchy through a royal decree.

On January 16, 2006, the Election Commission of Bhutan (ECB) was established to organise national elections including basic electoral education, promoting political awareness, and creating an effective voter registration system. It also held two mock elections to give the people a chance to familiarise themselves with the electoral mechanisms and the electronic voting machines. The democratisation process transformed the Bhutanese political system.

The first National Assembly elections in Bhutan took place on March 24, 2008. Two political parties contested in the landmark elections.

The Parliament of Bhutan has two houses: the National Council, which is a house of review, and the National Assembly. The National Council has 25 non-partisan members whereby the people elect 20 members, one for each of the 20 *dzongkhags* (districts), and the king appoints 5 eminent members. The members serve five-year terms.

The National Assembly has 47 members elected directly by the citizens through their constituencies. The leader of the party that wins majority seats in the National Assembly becomes the prime minister, also known as *lyonchhen*. The prime minister is supported by 10 cabinet ministers. All ministers must be natural-born citizens of Bhutan, and there is a limit of two ministers from any one *dzongkhag*.

On July 18, 2008, the fifth King, Jigme Khesar Namgyel Wangchuck, signed the Constitution, formally marking the end of a century of absolute monarchy in Bhutan.

Proverb

ཡེ་ཤེས་པའི་མདའ་ཆུབ་སར་མི་མཐོང་ཕོག་སར་མཐོང་།

Ye shey pi da chap sar mi thoeng; phog sar thoeng.

The arrow of the accomplished master will not be seen when it is released; only when it hits the target.

People and National Identity

Bhutan is remarkable in many ways. The Royal Government of Bhutan has prioritised sustaining both tangible and intangible aspects of its culture and national identity. Many unique elements bound the people together, from national dress to their world-class architectural design.

Just greet the Bhutanese with 'kuzuzangpo la' and you'll receive a warm smile in return

Demography of Bhutan

As of 2025, Bhutan has a population of around 798,000 people. The population density in Bhutan is 20 people per km² (52 people per mi²). 45.8% of the population live in urban areas (around 353,445 people) and the median age in Bhutan is 28.1 years old.

The country's inhabitants can be divided into three major ethnic groups: Ngalops in the west, Sharchops in the east and Lhotshampas in the south. However, Bhutanese are also collectively known as Drukpas, 'people from Bhutan'.

The Ngalops are Buddhists who originated from Tibet and primarily settled in the mountainous western region. In the 1850s, a group of Hindu foresters from Nepal migrated to Bhutan and began settling in the lowland regions of southern Bhutan. Thereafter, Indian and Nepalese workers were recruited to help implement the first Five-Year Plan in 1961. They are referred to as Lhotshampas, literally 'people from the southern border'. Meanwhile, the Sharchops are of mixed Tibetan, South Asian, and Southeast Asian descent that mostly live in the eastern districts of Bhutan.

In 1987, the fourth King, Jigme Singye Wangchuck, introduced the 'One Nation, One People' policy under the sixth Five-Year Plan to preserve and maintain the national identity of Bhutan. Subsequently, in 1989, as a part of this policy, he issued a *kasho* (royal decree) to promote *driglam namzha* (official code of etiquette and dress code), as well as the *Dzongkha* language to strengthen Bhutan's unique national identity.

Bhutanese are proud of their culture and traditions. It is visible in how they dress, their architecture, and their interdependence with the natural environment. Therefore, it is not surprising that cultural preservation is one of the main pillars of Bhutan's Gross National Happiness (GNH) philosophy.

Proverb

བསམ་པ་བཟང་ན་ས་དང་ལམ་ཡང་བཟང་། །བསམ་པ་ངན་ན་ས་དང་ལམ་ཡང་ངན།

Sampa zang na sa dang lam yang zang; sampa nyen na sa dang lam yang nyen.

If the thought is good, your place and path are good;
if the thought is bad, your place and path are bad.

Driglam Namzha

Driglam namzha, in essence, is the conduct of oneself. It focuses on certain physical, verbal and mental etiquette. It also emphasises good manners when alone or in the company of others. The practice of *driglam namzha* is a characteristic of the Bhutanese culture and identity. Every Bhutanese is taught the norms and practices from a young age and everyone is expected to have a basic understanding of it.

The history of this cultural etiquette dates back to the 17th century when Zhabdrung Ngawang Namgyal promoted the practices to establish order and unify the country. After the royal decree issued by the fourth King in 1989, *driglam namzha* became an official protocol, with a set of ceremonial conduct that is strictly adhered to by all citizens.

Ultimately, *driglam namzha* promotes values such as humility, self-control, and compassion while also displaying sensitivity and respect towards others. Some examples of behaviour include walking behind high officials, not sitting cross-legged in front of superiors, and bowing in the presence of the king or other high officials.

> **Driglam** means 'order, discipline, custom, rules, regimen'. **Namzha** means 'system'. *Driglam Namzha* governs how citizens dress in public and behave in official settings.

Bhutanese women looking beautiful in their bright *kiras* and *rachus*

National Dress

Bhutan's national dress is deemed very important for the preservation of its culture and national identity. Bhutanese take great pride in wearing their traditional clothing, and you can see them wearing the dress in daily life.

The traditional dress for men is the *gho*, a knee-length robe tied with a handwoven belt, known as *kera*. Under the *gho*, men wear a *tegu*, a white jacket with long, folded-back cuffs.

Women wear the *kira*, a large rectangular cloth held together by a *koma* (brooch). The *kira* is often worn with colourful blouses called *wonju* alongside a *tego* (an outer jacket).

The textiles are mostly handwoven and intricately designed by talented weavers throughout the country.

You can see the locals in their finest attires during special occasions such as weddings and festivals.

When visiting a *dzong* or government office flying the national flag, the Bhutanese wear the national dress with ceremonial scarves. Men will wear a *kabney* (silk scarf) from left shoulder to the hip, and women drape a *rachu*, a narrow embroidered cloth, over their left shoulder.

Bhutanese men looking suave in their ghos and white kabneys

Ceremonial Scarves in Bhutan

The rank of the person determines the colour of the *kabney* and *rachu* that a Bhutanese wears.

** Photos are for illustration purposes only. These are the more common scarfs that you'll see in Bhutan but there are other coloured scarfs that represent the different ranks.*

- Saffron - His Majesty the King and the Chief Abbot (*Je Khenpo*).
- Orange - Ministers.
- Red (*bura marp*) or Red-gold (*lungmar*) - *Dasho*, an honorary title conferred by the king.
- Green - Judges.
- Blue - Members of the National Assembly and National Council.
- White with fringes and a red band with one, two or three red stripes - District administrators and governors (*Dzongrab, Dungpa*).
- White with fringes and two broad, red, vertical borders (*khamar*) - Village chiefs (*Gups*).
- White for males and colourful for females - Commoner.

Bhutanese in their beautiful traditional dress are a common sight in Bhutan

Foreigners and tourists are not required to adhere to the strict dress code when entering the dzong, temples or monasteries but are required to dress decently such as tops with sleeves and long pants. However, you will need to remove your shoes and headgear.

Check out how to wear a full *kira*

s.bn.sg/kira

Livelihood

Bhutan remains a largely rural and agrarian economy. As in many developing countries, agro-pastoralism is the major form of livelihood for rural communities. As such, agriculture is the main livelihood for more than half of the Bhutanese population.

The majority of the Bhutanese live in small rural villages along the mountainous ridges and river valleys. Traditionally they were a subsistence farming population, largely self-sufficient in food: growing their own crops and grazing animals for meat, butter, cheese and milk. Work is often communal, and there is usually a cooperative environment in the village to help farmers sow and harvest their crops.

The other primary sources of income for Bhutanese are tourism, hydropower and public sectors, including civil service, government agencies and the armed forces.

A Bhutanese woman removing chaff from rice using the traditional method

Houses and Architecture

Houses in Bhutan are traditionally built with stone, wood and rammed earth that may rise as high as three storeys. Lively and colourful motifs adorn the homes.

The traditional houses are an architectural feat as they are constructed entirely without nails, just like their magnificent fortresses. Heavy stones hold the shingled roofs to prevent them from being swept away by strong winds. Windows are made up of sliding panels, and narrow stairs connect one floor to the next. The ground floor houses domestic animals and a storage area, while the first floor is the living quarters and kitchen.

The top floor is the most important part of the house. There is usually a *choesum*, an elaborately decorated shrine room with an altar.

With modernisation, building materials became readily available. The new houses are made up of cement, bricks, stones and sand, and the roofs of corrugated galvanised iron sheets.

You can also find thatched bamboo houses in the lower altitudes in the southern region of Bhutan. Meanwhile, the semi-nomadic yak herders in the northern region live in tiny stone houses or yak-hair tents as they move across the pasture land.

Designs of traditional buildings in Bhutan must adhere to strict cultural guidelines

A traditional Bhutanese house with idyllic surroundings in Chumey, Bumthang

Food and Drink

Bhutanese cuisine is influenced by Chinese, Tibetan and Indian cuisines. However, as Bhutanese food habits and dishes continue to evolve, Bhutan develops its own distinctive flavours.

Contrary to popular belief, not all Bhutanese are vegetarians. A large part of the population still enjoys eating meat even though Bhutan is a predominantly Buddhist country.

Beef and **pork** as air dried meats are commonly served in Bhutan, and **yak meat** from the highlanders is a delicacy. Fish are rare in Bhutan as there are strict regulations on fishing in the country but farmed freshwater trout is becoming popular.

Some popular meat dishes include **shakam paa** (dried beef), **sikkam paa** (desiccated thin sliced pork) and **jasha maru** (chicken stew).

A common ingredient that runs through most Bhutanese food is **chilli peppers.** While you are in Bhutan, expect to see bright red peppers drying on roofs under the sun.

Bhutanese eat many plant-based foods such as wild mushrooms, sweet potatoes, tender bamboo shoots, fiddlehead ferns, nettle flowers, and orchid flower buds.

Some authentic Bhutanese dishes that you can find in a staple diet include a mountain of rice, usually healthy red rice, **ema datshi** (chilli cheese), and **ezay** (chilli condiment).

Ema datshi is a traditional Bhutanese stew made up of ema (chillies) and datshi (yak cheese). It is deemed the national dish of Bhutan, and is loved by both locals and tourists alike. **Kewa datshi (**potato cheese) and **shamu datshi** (mushroom cheese) are other delicious Bhutanese dishes.

A popular breakfast choice in Bhutan is **khur-le** (buckwheat pancake). Meanwhile, during winter, **bathuk** (wheat flour noodle soup) is a favourite for Bhutanese to keep themselves warm.

Just like the Nepalis, Bhutanese also enjoy eating steamed dumplings, locally known as **momos.** You can easily find meat or vegetable dumplings all over the country.

You can also find garlands of **chugo** (hardened cheese) hanging outside grocery stores. Chugo is made from yak's milk, air-dried until it becomes hard like a rock. Don't worry if you have difficulty sucking chugo; it is known to be the hardest cheese in the world!

Some Bhutanese also love chewing **doma** (areca nut) wrapped in betel leaves with a dash of slaked lime after a meal. Doma is addictive for its stimulant effects. It is an acquired taste, somewhat bitter, and chewing too much of it can turn your teeth and lips red. The locals may offer you doma as a customary greeting, or polite social gesture.

Suja (butter tea) is often served on all social occasions along with some **zaw** (roasted rice). **Ara** — a spirit distilled from rice, maize, wheat or barley — is also one of the Bhutanese's favourite beverages.

There are also locally produced alcoholic beverages such as Red Panda, Druk 11000, Bhutanese Red-Rice Lager and more. Many alcohol lovers sing praises for the Zumzin peach wine and K5 whiskeys.

Bhutan is a paradise for spicy food lovers

Doma is the culprit for all the red-stained teeth

Chicken stew is a popular Bhutanese dish

Tea time usually means butter tea and roasted rice

Try biting into the hardest cheese in the world

Savour the taste of dried pork with chillies

Traditional Eating Habits in Bhutan

Mealtimes are social affairs in Bhutan. When eating in a group, Bhutanese traditionally observe the *driglam namzha* and are expected to sit cross-legged in a circle on the floor. In the past, the head of the family is served first, and no one can leave until all the family members finish eating.

Silence is to be maintained while eating. However, these traditional practices are fading over time. These days, mealtimes are no longer quiet, and laughter is shared instead.

Traditionally, dishes were served in dapas (wooden bowls), but with the easy availability of modern goods, modern ceramic bowls have replaced the wooden bowls. Similarly, *bangchungs* — circular containers made from special bamboo called *yura* — were also used to serve rice and other dry snacks. Bhutanese rarely use these traditional products now, but you can still find conventional dapas or *bangchungs* sold in many handicraft shops.

Back in the day, Bhutanese used to eat with their hands while sitting on the floor. With modernisation, eating habits have changed and evolved. In urban areas, Bhutanese usually eat with cutleries and on regular dining tables. Nowadays, you will usually find Bhutanese eating with their hands only when they are at home or having a picnic.

Stir-fried noodles is an Asian delicacy

The locals enjoy eating pork dishes

Potato cheese in Bhutan is a must-try

Chilli cheese is a celebrated dish in Bhutan

Buckwheat dumplings are a unique local specialty

Religions, Customs and Traditions

> **"** While Buddhism is widely practiced in Bhutan, about 20% of the population practice Hinduism, especially amongst the Lhotshampas. Christians are present in small numbers. **"**

Buddhism in Bhutan

Bhutan is the only country in the world where Vajrayana Buddhism, known as the 'Thunderbolt Vehicle' or 'Diamond Vehicle', is practiced as the state religion. Ever since Buddhism was introduced to the country, religion has been very prevalent in every facet of Bhutanese life. Buddhist values are often inculcated in the younger generations during their formative years.

Buddhism originated from the teachings of Siddharta Gautama, also known as Shakyamuni Buddha, a royal prince from the Shakya clan in the 6th century BCE. When Gautama stumbled upon human sufferings outside of his palace, he renounced all worldly pleasures and embarked on a spiritual quest to seek solutions to the suffering. After years of rigorous contemplation and meditation, he gained enlightenment while meditating under a ficus tree, known as 'The Bodhi Tree'.

Following the Buddha's passing, different schools of thought appeared amongst his disciples, influencing their interpretation of the doctrines. There are two principal schools of Buddhism, Mahayana and Hinayana — sometimes referred to as Theravada.

In addition, Vajrayana (tantrism) emerged as a branch of Mahayana teachings. Over the centuries, Vajrayana in Tibet gradually divided into four major schools: Nyingmapa, Kagyupa, Sakyapa and Gelugpa. Nyingmapa is the oldest sect that traces its origin back to the teachings of the great Indian saint Guru Padmasambhava, popularly known as Guru Rinpoche.

Buddhist teachings of compassion are the basis for Bhutanese religious beliefs and practices. The majority of the Bhutanese population follow either the Drukpa Kagyu or Nyingma sect. The people in central and eastern Bhutan widely follow Nyingmapa, whereas the people from the western region practice Drukpa Kagyu.

Prayer wheels are inscribed with sacred mantras

Spinning the prayer wheels can bring enlightenment to all sentient beings

It's common for monks to join the monastery at a very young age

The offering of butter lamps is a usual spiritual practice for Bhutanese

The sight of fluttering colourful prayer flags in Bhutan has a calming effect

Monks play the *dungchen* — a long horn or trumpet — during ceremonies

Guru Rinpoche

An Indian Tantric Master Padmasambhava, popularly known as 'Guru Rinpoche', is one of Bhutan's most important historical and religious figures. His first visit to Bumthang in 746 AD is considered a turning point in the country's history and the actual introduction of Vajrayana Buddhism to Bhutan.

The King of Bumthang invited Guru Rinpoche to visit his land to subdue and tame demons, subsequently converting them to deities who protect the different valleys in Bhutan. You can find statues of Guru Rinpoche in almost all the Bhutanese temples throughout the country built after his first visit.

He is said to have eight manifestations and personifies the guru principle — known as the 'Second Buddha' — as prophesied by Sakyamuni, the historical Buddha. He is also regarded as the founder of the Nyingma school, the oldest religious sect of Vajrayana Buddhism. Guru Rinpoche preserved his teachings and wisdom by concealing *terma* (hidden treasures) in caves, rocks, and lakes to be discovered by future tertons (treasure revealers). One of the most important tertons in Bhutan is Pema Lingpa, who found many statues, scrolls and sacred relics during his time.

Guru Rinpoche visited Bhutan a second time via Singye Dzong in Lhuentse in eastern Bhutan. He left a body print and an impression of his head with a hat at Gom Kora in Trashiyangtse, eastern Bhutan. He flew in the form of Dorje Drolö, one of his eight manifestations, on the back of a flaming tigress to Taktsang in Paro, giving the famous monastery the name 'Tiger's Nest'. The monastery is one of Guru Rinpoche's most sacred sites as he concealed many profound treasures at Taktsang.

A huge statue of Guru Rinpoche in Lhuentse

Guru Rinpoche was often represented in his manifestation as Padmasambhava, wearing the dark blue gown of a mantra practitioner, the red and yellow shawl of a monk, the maroon cloak of a king, and the red robe and white undergarments of a bodhisattva.

Snow-covered Taktsang Monastery during winter season

The Drukpa Kagyu

The eminent religious master Tsangpa Gyare Yeshe Dorje, one of the foremost disciples of Lingje Repa Pema Dorje, founded the Drukpa Kagyu school at the Ralung monastery in Tibet during the 12th century.

Phajo Drugom Zhigpo fulfilled Tsangpa Gyare's prophecy that a young man from eastern Tibet would travel south to spread the Drukpa Kagyu teachings in western Bhutan.

After that, many Buddhist scholars visited Bhutan, but Zhabdrung Ngawang Namgyal's arrival in 1616 established Drukpa Kagyu as the state religion.

Young monks mingling outside the temple

Feel free to interact with the young monks

Women sometimes pray while spinning the wheel

Painting of a phallus on the wall of a handicraft shop

Lama Drukpa Kuenley

Of the numerous saints and scholars who visited Bhutan over the centuries, the Tibetan lama Drukpa Kuenley, from the Drukpa Kagyu lineage, is a popular Buddhist yogi in Bhutanese history.

People remember him for his unorthodox and unconventional teaching methods — usually with bizarre sexual connotations. His 'crazy wisdom' earned him the name 'Divine Madman'.

He was known for using his phallus to awaken unenlightened beings and to subdue demons. Drukpa Kuenley's phallus was so powerful that it is known as the 'Thunderbolt of Flaming Wisdom'. Devotees flock to Chimi Lhakhang, a monastery established to honour Drukpa Kuenley, to offer prayers — many praying specifically for children.

The phallus is now the symbolic reference of fertility and good luck and is a common sight on walls of houses, particularly in western Bhutan. The embellished images are also said to ward off evil spirits.

People from all over the world visit Chimi Lhakhang in Punakha to receive fertility blessings. Many modern miracle babies, sometimes named Chimi or Kinley, have been conceived after their parents received the fertility blessings.

Visit **www.chimelhakang.com** for more information

The Nyingmapa

The Nyingmapa lineage is the oldest of the major schools of Tibetan Buddhism. It traces its origin to Padmasambhava, who travelled to Tibet at Tibetan King Trisong Deutsen's invitation to help the King establish Buddhism there.

Padmasambhava travelled to Tibet with Shantarakshita, a renowned Buddhist scholar. In Tibet, he pacified the demons, turned them into Dharma protectors and successfully established Buddhism.Padmasambhava had 25 disciples to whom he transmitted the Vajrayana teachings. A vast and complex system of transmission lineages developed from his disciples.

In the early years, the Nyingmapa lineage did not have any proper structure. It relied on oral transmission from master to disciple. The lineage gradually became more institutionalised, and by the 15th century, Tibet had established many monasteries. An important aspect of the Nyingmapa lineage is the transmission of teachings through *terma* (hidden treasures).

Padmasambhava brought Buddhism to Bhutan in the 8th century and established numerous sacred sites that are important pilgrimage sites today.

There are many types of prayer wheels in Bhutan

ཁ་བདེཕ་གུ་ཕྱེ་བདེཕ་མ་སྐྱལ།

Kha deu gu chey deu ma kay.

Don't put an easy tongue upon an easy mouth.

Hidden treasures were discovered in the famous Burning Lake of Bumthang

Hinduism in Bhutan

While Bhutanese are predominantly Buddhists, the Lhotshampa community in the south are of Nepali and Indian descent who practice Hinduism. Hindus in Bhutan are estimated to be around 20% of the population. Hinduism is one of the world's oldest religions, and its earliest teachings are found in scriptures known as Vedas. The Vedas are amongst the oldest sacred religious texts.

Hinduism has very diverse views on the concept of God. There are six major schools of orthodox Indian Hindu philosophy — Nyaya, Vaisheshika, Samkhya, Yoga, Mīmāṃsā and Vedanta.

The major schools of Hindu philosophy explain morality and the nature of existence through the doctrines of *samsara*, the continuous cycle of life, death and reincarnation, and *karma*, the universal law of cause and effect. Major Hindu festivals are national holidays in Bhutan.

Devi Panchayan Mandir in Thimphu

When visiting religious buildings

You should observe a few important rules when visiting a *lhakhang* (temple) or *goemba* (monastery).

- You are required to remove your footwear and headgear at the doorway.

- Photography is prohibited inside the temple.

- Ensure that you are dressed appropriately — avoid shorts or sleeveless tops.

- Always move in a clockwise direction when circumambulating a stupa (sacred shrine), chorten (religious structure) or prayer wheel.

- It is customary to leave a small monetary offering on the altar. You should touch the note to your forehead and then place it on the altar. A monk may pour some holy water from a sacred vessel called *bumpa*, into your hand. You can take a sip of the water and then spread the rest on your head, sweeping from front to back.

- Do not point at any deity, statues, religious artefacts or paintings as it is considered disrespectful. Instead, use an open-palm gesture with your palm up.

- While male visitors may be permitted to enter the goenkhang (inner sanctum), always ask your tour guide before entering. Women are not allowed to enter a goenkhang.

Economy of Bhutan

Bhutan has one of the world's smallest economies. They have sustained growth due to the development of the hydroelectric sector and the dynamism of the tourism sector. Bhutan is also the first country to use the Gross National Happiness (GNH) index to measure the country's development and progress.

Bhutan's Economy

Significant sectors of Bhutan's economy today consist of forestry, tourism, and hydroelectric power sales. Bhutan also exports cement, dolomite, ferroalloys, agricultural products, handicrafts, and cordyceps sinensis. The rural economy is still primarily based on subsistence agriculture.

Bhutan has one of the world's smallest economies, with the 2023 Gross Domestic Product at around USD2.69bn. Bhutan has an average GDP growth of 7.5%. The hydroelectricity and construction sectors generally contribute over one-third of the GDP, while the rest come from the service and primary sectors.

Bhutan has invested heavily in hydroelectricity to become self-sufficient, intending to generate about 10,000 megawatts of hydropower.

The government actively encourages the development of other sectors, such as waste management, education services, healthcare services and information technology.

There has also been a deliberate focus on attracting foreign investments into several sectors through foreign direct investment (FDI).

Bhutan successfully met the Least Developed Countries (LDCs) graduation criteria in two United Nations triennial reviews of 2015 and 2018 and has graduated from the group of LDCs in December 2023.

This marks Bhutan as the seventh nation to graduate from the band of Least Developed Countries set up by the United Nations (UN) in 1971.

A tourist browsing through a handicraft shop

A tourist learning about Bhutan's traditional crafts

A key challenge is the rising youth unemployment. The government has implemented various schemes to support young people: expanding their skill set, identifying avenues for employment, promoting entrepreneurship education, and encouraging self-employment.

Currency

The financial services sector is also evolving. There are four central banks and multiple insurance companies.

The Bank of Bhutan, with headquarters in Phuentsholing, was established by a Royal Charter in 1968, a significant step towards the transition from barter to an entirely monetary system. Today, the Bank of Bhutan has many branches throughout the country.

In 1974, Bhutan introduced the Ngultrum (BTN) as the official currency. The Ngultrum is on par with the Indian Rupee and available in the following denominations: Nu. 1, Nu. 5, Nu. 10, Nu. 20, Nu. 50, Nu. 100, Nu. 500, Nu. 1,000.

You are encouraged to bring larger denominations for exchange as larger bills will give you a higher exchange rate. Check out the FAQs (pg. 240) for the currencies that you can exchange in Bhutan. Do note that US Dollar bills issued before the year 2000 are not accepted. Indian Rupees (INR50, INR100 and INR500) are commonly accepted in Bhutan.

Tourism

Tourism in Bhutan is still relatively young; the kingdom first opened its doors to foreign tourists in 1974. In that year, Bhutan received a total of a mere 287 foreign visitors.

However, the tourism industry in the kingdom is vibrant and holds high potential for growth. Bhutan's tourism is founded on the principle of sustainability, where tourism must be environmentally and ecologically friendly, socially and culturally acceptable, and economically viable.

Thus, sustainability lies at the core of the 'High value, Low volume' tourism policy implementation. This differentiation from other destinations serves as a competitive advantage for Bhutan as a high-end travel destination.

As part of this policy, the government has implemented a Sustainable Development Fee (SDF), which is a tourism levy imposed on all leisure tourists.

All tourists, except nationals from India, are required to pay an SDF of USD 100 (children aged 6 to 11 – USD 50) per person per night. Children aged 5 and below are exempted from the SDF. The SDF contributes towards sustainable development initiatives aimed at enhancing the tourist experience.

Regional tourists from India are required to apply for a permit and pay an SDF of 1200 INR per person per night.

Do note that the SDF does not cover your accommodation, meals, guide, or driver. As of September 2022, tourists are no longer required to book their trips to Bhutan through a tour operator. However, why stress yourself when visiting the Kingdom of Happiness?

Booking a tour package from a reputable tour operator remains the most cost-effective and efficient way to experience the magic of Bhutan due to the limited public transport infrastructure.

Why do you pay the Sustainable Development Fee (SDF)?

1. To contribute to the overall sustainability of tourism in Bhutan.

2. To contribute to the enhancement of infrastructure and facilities, particularly the tourism infrastructure and facilities.

3. To process route permits in advance so that tourists do not have to wait at the border gates when visiting the different districts.

4. To ensure the safety of all tourists through dedicated tour guides.

5. To get preferential exemptions from paying entry fees for state-owned tourist attractions.

6. To receive guaranteed quality services from the hospitality and tourism sector.

The picturesque Phobjikha Valley is well-loved by many tourists

Eastern Bhutan is a paradise for offbeat travellers

Education

Until the 1950s, the form of education available in Bhutan was mainly monastic. The growing influence of the British in the late 19th century influenced Ugyen Wangchuck towards Western-style education. He set up private schools in Haa and Bumthang. Today, there are three primary forms of education in Bhutan: general education, monastic education and non-formal education. General education is currently seen as the formal education structure.

The government encourages Bhutanese to pursue education and provides **free education** to every child of school age. In addition, the government also provides university scholarships to students who excel in their studies.

From 1961 to 2020, the modern education system has expanded from about 11 schools to 1132 schools, including early childhood education, primary schools, secondary schools, technical and vocational institutions, as well as tertiary institutions.

Increasingly, many efforts are focused on providing technical and vocational training to the youths. The government believes that equipping students with relevant skills will help ensure employability in the future.

Bhutan's youth literacy rate (15 - 24 years old) is at 84%, and English has been the medium of instruction since the beginning of modern education.

> As a result, most Bhutanese are fluent in English, especially the younger generation.

Bhutanese students enjoy free education in the country

Technology

Unlike most countries that gradually experience technological progression, technology advancement happened rapidly in Bhutan. The kingdom was one of the last countries in the world to introduce television and the Internet in 1999. Given the global trends, the decision to establish technological infrastructure and services was inevitable. Currently, more than 87% of the population has a cell phone.

Recognising the importance of technology, the fifth King constantly emphasises the need to promote technology literacy and skills in Bhutan.

The government inaugurated the first IT park in Thimphu in May 2012. Thimphu Tech Park is the first of its kind in the kingdom. There is also an incubation centre within the park where entrepreneurs can run pilot tests to harness any technology opportunity for Bhutan.

Healthcare

As with education, Bhutan provides **free health care** services to its citizens. Bhutan established modern health care in the early 1960s and since then has made remarkable progress, with more than 90% of the population benefiting from primary health care services. Basic health units (BHU) and outreach clinics bring health care to remote areas. Patients in need of sophisticated and expensive treatments are referred abroad at the government's expense.

The current life expectancy in Bhutan is 72.17 years. In 2024, the infant mortality rate for Bhutan Is 19.57 deaths per 1,000 live births, a 2.86% decline from 2023. Bhutan has made major progress in lowering the infant mortality rate. Child immunisation is above 90%, and access to potable water and public sanitation has improved over the years. The government invests a major proportion of its expenditure in education and healthcare.

Bhutan organised the first Startup Weekend in 2016

Primary health care services are free in Bhutan

Gross National Happiness

Most people have probably heard of Bhutan because of its development vision of Gross National Happiness (GNH). This concept was announced by the fourth King, Jigme Singye Wangchuck, in 1979. He believes that happiness should be the goal for human progress instead of GDP.

GNH strives to measure development more holistically, focusing on balancing the people's physical, spiritual, emotional and psychological well-being.

In establishing the GNH Index, Bhutan created a metric to measure the quality of life in terms of happiness.

GNH is perceived as four pillars: good governance, sustainable socio-economic development, cultural preservation and environmental conservation. These are expanded into nine domains, 38 sub-indexes, 72 indicators (33 grouped indicators), and 151 variables to define and analyse the happiness of the Bhutanese.

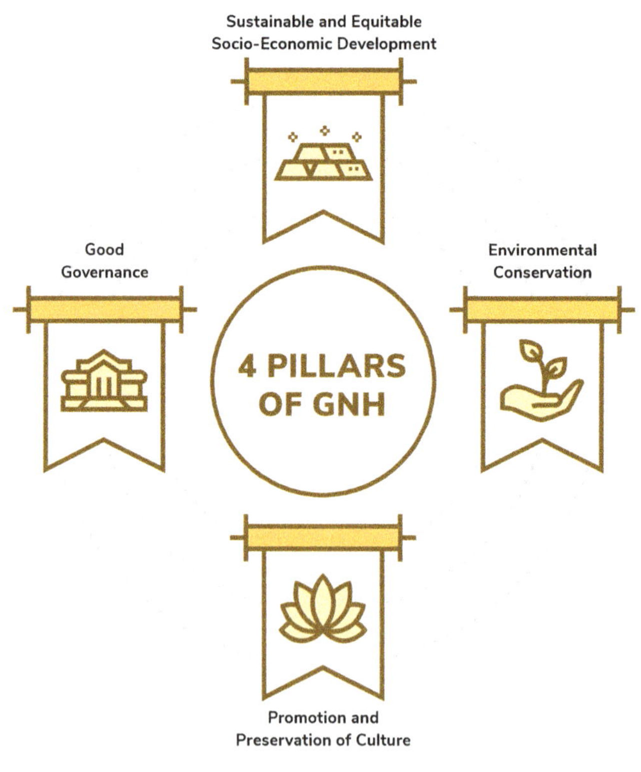

Bhutan carefully plans and executes surveys on five-year cycles in line with its tradition of presenting five-year plans. In the past, the survey could take up to nine hours to complete. They have now condensed it to three hours.

In Bhutan, all government policies and development plans have to align with the fundamental tenets of GNH.

The Gross National Happiness Commission (GNHC) is the government agency tasked with incorporating GNH into policy-making and planning.

In line with the GNH pillars, Bhutan is a world leader in environmental preservation. The kingdom currently holds the title of being the **world's only carbon-negative country.** It absorbs more greenhouse gases in the atmosphere than it emits.

The constitution of Bhutan also mandates that the country maintain a minimum forest cover of 60%. Currently, over 70% of the land is covered by forests, making Bhutan one of the greenest countries in the world.

Festivals of Bhutan

Festivals are one of the most important aspects of Bhutanese culture. The kingdom is famous for its exuberant religious festivals. These special celebrations carry a lot of spiritual significance for the locals.

A dancer wearing a mask of a mythical creature

Tshechus

Every year, thousands of visitors flock to Bhutan's various dzongs to experience the *tshechus*

Tshechu literally means 'tenth day' and is considered the most important religious festival in Bhutan. It is held annually in the monasteries and *dzongs* of all the 20 districts. In the different months of the year, the festival honours Guru Rinpoche, who brought Buddhism to Bhutan in the 8th century.

A *tshechu* typically lasts for four or five days. It is celebrated on the tenth day of the Bhutanese lunar calendar, corresponding to the birthday of Guru Rinpoche. Hence, the exact dates of the *tshechu* in the different districts vary from year to year.

For Bhutanese, attending this religious festival is an integral part of their spiritual devotion to Buddhism. They believe that by attending the festival, they can accumulate spiritual merits and move towards enlightenment, the ultimate goal of Buddhism. Today, *tshechus* are also important social events in every district.

Tips

The popular tshechus for tourists to attend are Paro Tshechu during spring and Thimphu Tshechu and Bumthang Tshechu during autumn.

Cham (Dance)

The highlight of the festival is the sacred *Cham* performances by both laity and monks dressed in ornate costumes. The ancient dances have been transmitted in Bhutan from person-to-person, for hundreds of years. Young monks undergo an extensive apprenticeship to learn the precise steps and positions for the performance.

The dancers perform evocative titles like 'Dance of the Lords of Cremation Grounds', 'Dance of the Terrifying Deities', etc. While members of the community perform folk dances and music, the *Cham* are performances by monks who regard the performance as a spiritual practice.

Ritual music is played using cymbal, drum, flute, and yak-horn to accompany the dances. Dancers usually wear wooden masks that represent animals and fearsome deities. The *tshechu* festival held over several days often ends with a dance dedicated to the eight manifestations of Guru Rinpoche. The most distinctive mask represents the wrathful manifestation of Guru Rinpoche, which he transformed into to tame harmful deities.

The dances re-enact the events that took place during the life of Padmasambhava, mostly depicting goodness triumphing over evil. The Bhutanese believe that just by observing the sacred dances, they will be blessed, enlightened and purified.

Each dancer visualise their body as a divine being

Each dance performance requires meticulous efforts

The Atsara is a cultural icon

Atsaras

The Atsara — a comical character in a red mask and a big phallus on top of his head — plays a vital role in Bhutanese festivals. These humorous figures are often associated with clowns due to their wittiness and burlesque appearance at tshechus. However, these Atsara figures are more than clowns for entertainment. The Atsara holds the responsibility of being the master of ceremony to ensure that the festival runs smoothly and, more importantly, helps the audience put their worries behind. In modern times, the Atsara also plays the role of an advocate to educate the masses on important issues such as personal well-being and hygiene.

The term 'Atsara' originated from the Sanskrit word acārya (holy Indian masters). Thus, we can say that the Atsara is a teacher who reminds the audience to let go of their inhibitions and unleash their free spirit.

Several Atsaras provide comic relief at the annual festivals

Latest Festival Calendar

s.bn.sg/bhutanfest

The Unfurling of a *Thongdrel*

Thongdrel means 'liberation at sight'. The final act of any *tshechu* festival is the unfurling of a *thongdrel*, a huge appliqué *thangka* often the size of a wall at a monastery.

These giant religious scrolls depicting images of Guru Rinpoche and various spiritual deities are so sacred that Bhutanese believe the mere sight of it can purify obstacles and help them accumulate great merits.

Typically, the Bhutanese unfurl the *thongdrel* at an early hour in the morning — around 3 to 4am — and roll it up by 7.30am to avoid direct sunlight on the *thongdrel*.

Bhutanese seek blessings from a silk appliqué *throngdel* of Guru Rinpoche at the end of a festival

Trekking in Bhutan

In eastern Bhutan, traditional Bhutanese houses are built with stones

Trails in Bhutan

Bhutan is home to some of the most magnificent Himalayan trails, including the most challenging high-altitude treks in the world. The mountains of Bhutan offer unspoiled and uncrowded wilderness experiences with incredible views of the Himalayan peaks. Trekking in Bhutan is also one of the most exciting and unforgettable ways to experience the kingdom.

Whether you are an experienced hiker or a novice, you will find trails in Bhutan that suit your fitness level.

Bhutan offers treks of various durations. There are short treks ranging from a few days to month-long expeditions.

The kingdom is also in the midst of reviving an ancient trail formerly used by armies and traders for thousands of years. Soon, you'll be able to embark on the Trans Bhutan Trail, an exhilarating long-distance trail traversing mountain ridges, lush valleys and dozens of quaint towns and villages.

For more information, check out **www.bhutantreks.com.**

Trekking Season

Jan	Feb	Mar	Apr	May	Jun	Jul	Aug	Sep	Oct	Nov	Dec
		Bumdra Trek (7 days)						Bumdra Trek (7 days)			
		Jomolhari Trek (7 or 11 days)									
		Druk Path (9 days)									
		Dagala Thousand Lakes Trek (9 days)									
		Rodung La Trek (9 days)									
						Salt Trek (9 days)					
		Royal Manas Trek (10 days)						Royal Manas Trek (10 days)			
		Samtengang Trek (11 days)									
		Merak-Sakteng Trek (18 days)						Merak-Sakteng Trek (18 days)			
		Laya-Gasa Trek (21 days)									
		Lunana Snowman Trek (28 days)									
		Trans Bhutan Trail Trek (37 days)									

*Between mid-June and mid-September, you should expect regular rainfall.

Difficulty level

● Average   ● High   ● Ultra High

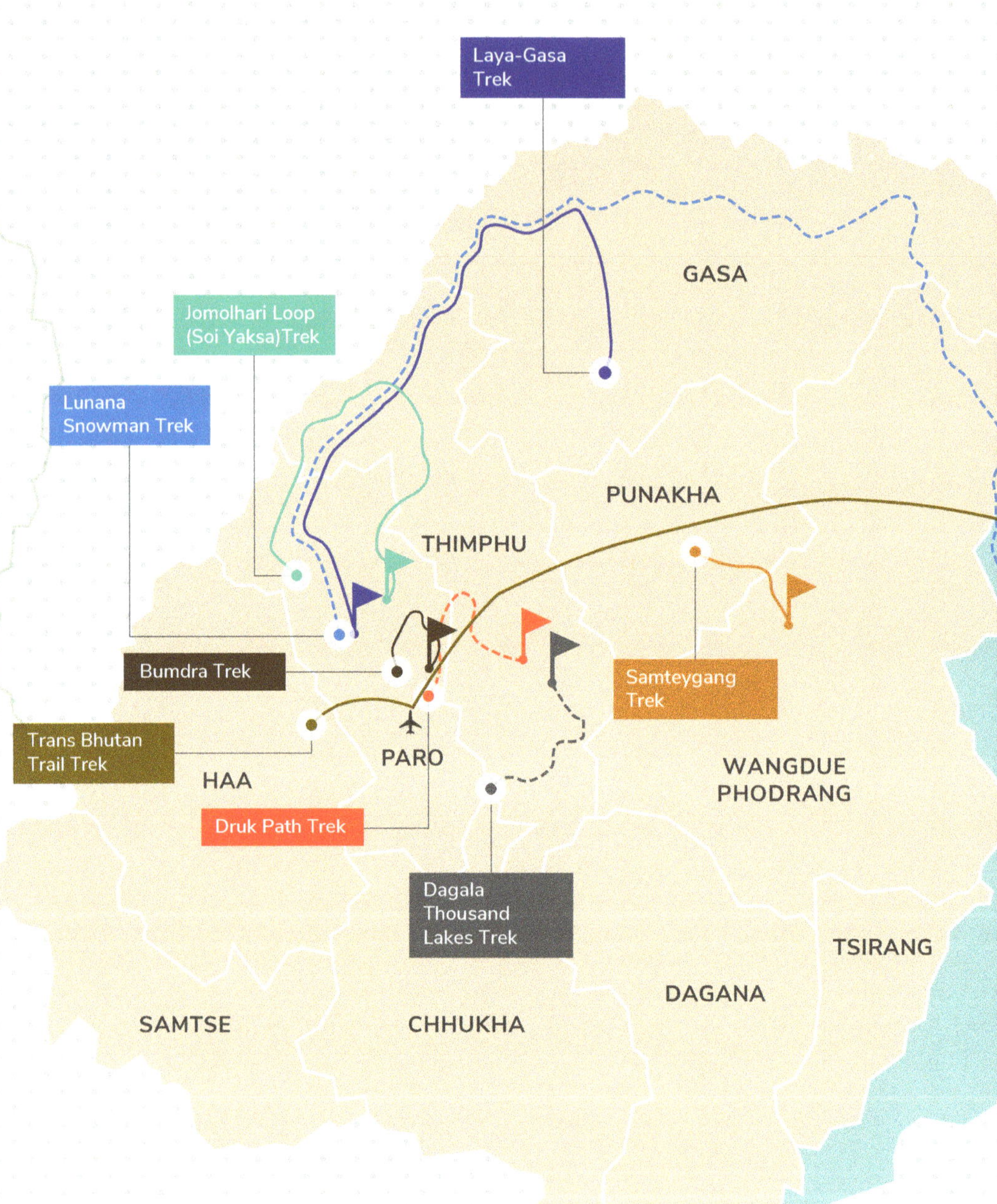

Laya-Gasa Trek
Jomolhari Loop (Soi Yaksa)Trek
Lunana Snowman Trek
GASA
PUNAKHA
THIMPHU
Bumdra Trek
Trans Bhutan Trail Trek
HAA
Druk Path Trek
PARO
Samteygang Trek
WANGDUE PHODRANG
Dagala Thousand Lakes Trek
TSIRANG
DAGANA
SAMTSE
CHHUKHA

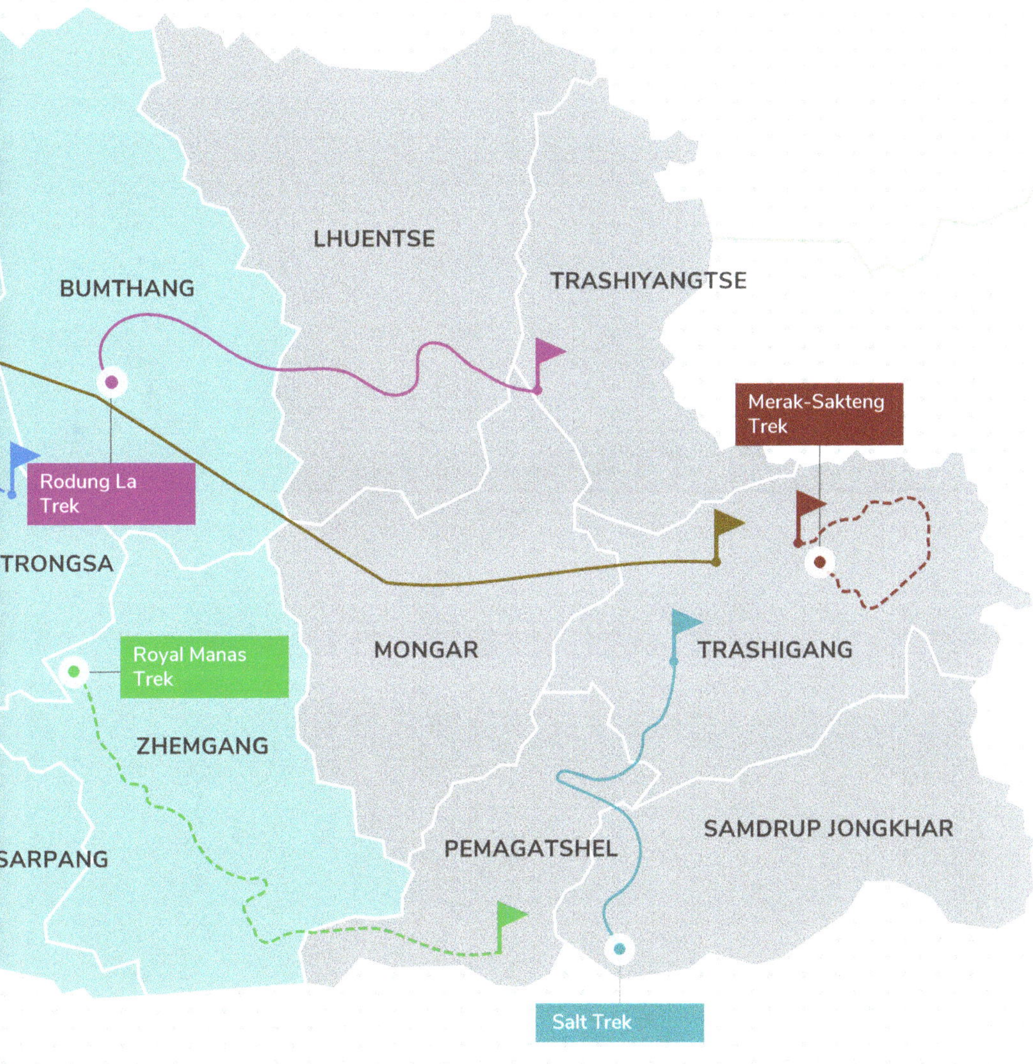

Bhutan Trekking Map
Start
End
Trails
Paro Airport
TIBET (AUTONOMOUS REGION OF CHINA)
LHUENTSE
TRASHIYANGTSE
BUMTHANG
Merak-Sakteng Trek
Rodung La Trek
TRONGSA
Royal Manas Trek
MONGAR
TRASHIGANG
ZHEMGANG
SARPANG
PEMAGATSHEL
SAMDRUP JONGKHAR
Salt Trek
INDIA

Bumdra Trek

7 DAYS

Difficulty level:	Moderate
Max elevation:	3,900 m
Min elevation:	2,800 m
Season:	Feb to May, Sep to Nov
Start from:	Sang Choekor
End at:	Ramthangkha

Huddle around a bonfire at night with your camping buddies for memories that'll last you a lifetime

Bumdra Trek, also known as 'Trek of Thousand Dakinis', is Bhutan's most beautiful short-duration trek, with one night of camping in the wilderness. It's the ideal trek if you love nature yet do not have much time in Bhutan. The views and sceneries along the way are breathtaking. You will also get a spectacular view of the iconic landmark of Bhutan — Taktsang Monastery, aka Tiger's Nest Monastery — from the top!

Highlights

- Sightseeing in Thimphu, Punakha and Paro
- Visit Sang Choekhor Shedra, a Buddhist college
- Visit the iconic Taktsang Monastery (Tiger's Nest Monastery)

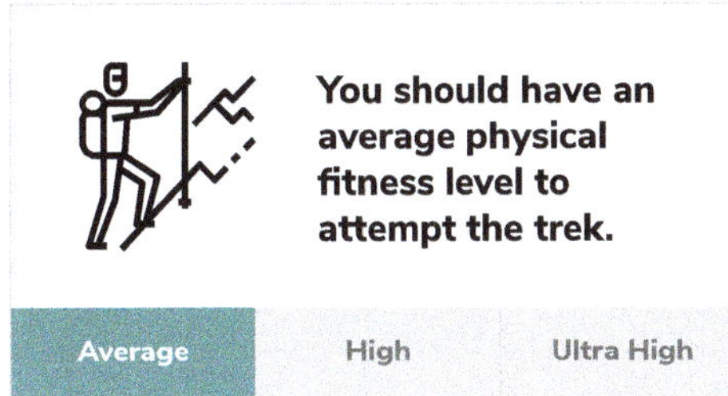

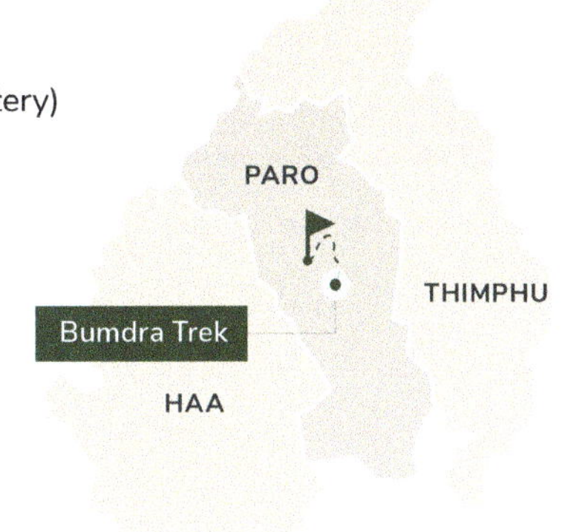

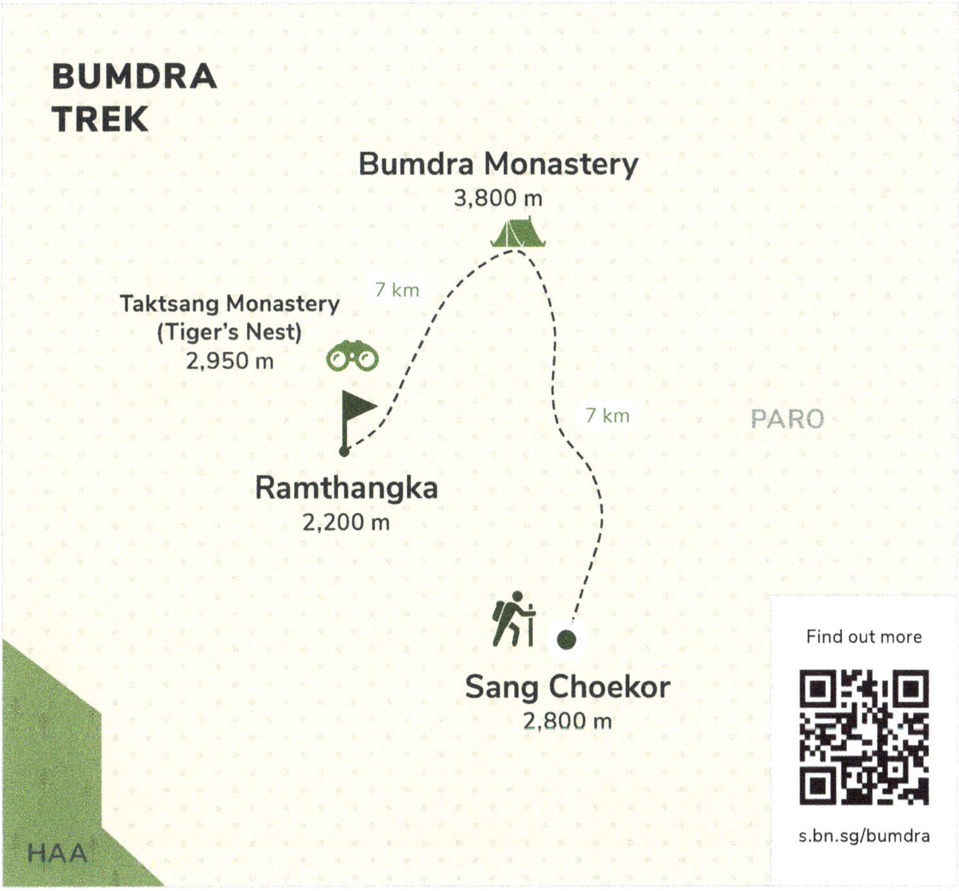

BUMDRA TREK

Camp overnight in the wilderness while enjoying the view of the spectacular mountains

Dagala Thousand Lakes Trek

9 DAYS

Difficulty level:	Moderate
Max elevation:	4,720 m
Min elevation:	2,250 m
Season:	March to October
Start from:	Geynikha Village
End at:	Chamgang

Stunning views of the Himalayan mountains and pristine lakes

The trek begins in Geynikha village and takes you through pristine and crystal-clear lakes. You will see exquisite wildflowers and gaze at the spectacular Himalayan range. Expect to see mountains like Mt Everest, Mt Jomolhari, Masang Gang, Jichu Drake, and Gangche Ta. You will also traverse through several quaint Bhutanese villages and experience an authentic village lifestyle.

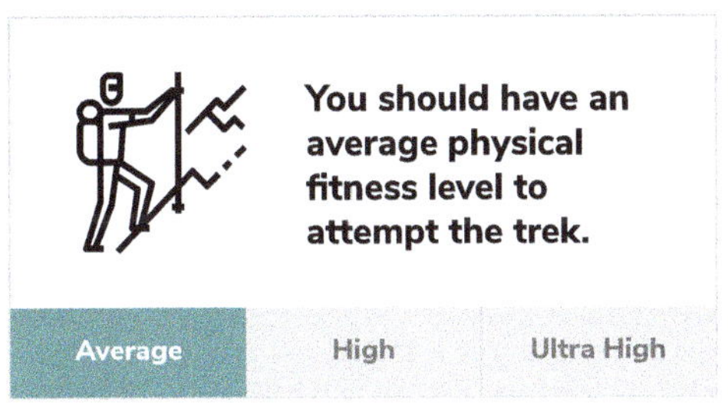

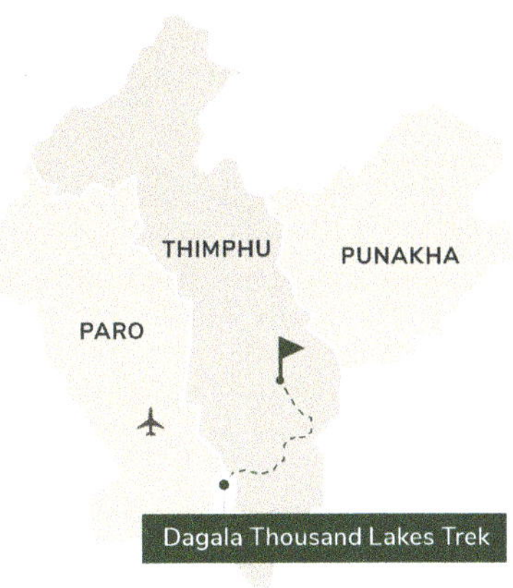

DAGALA THOUSAND LAKES TREK

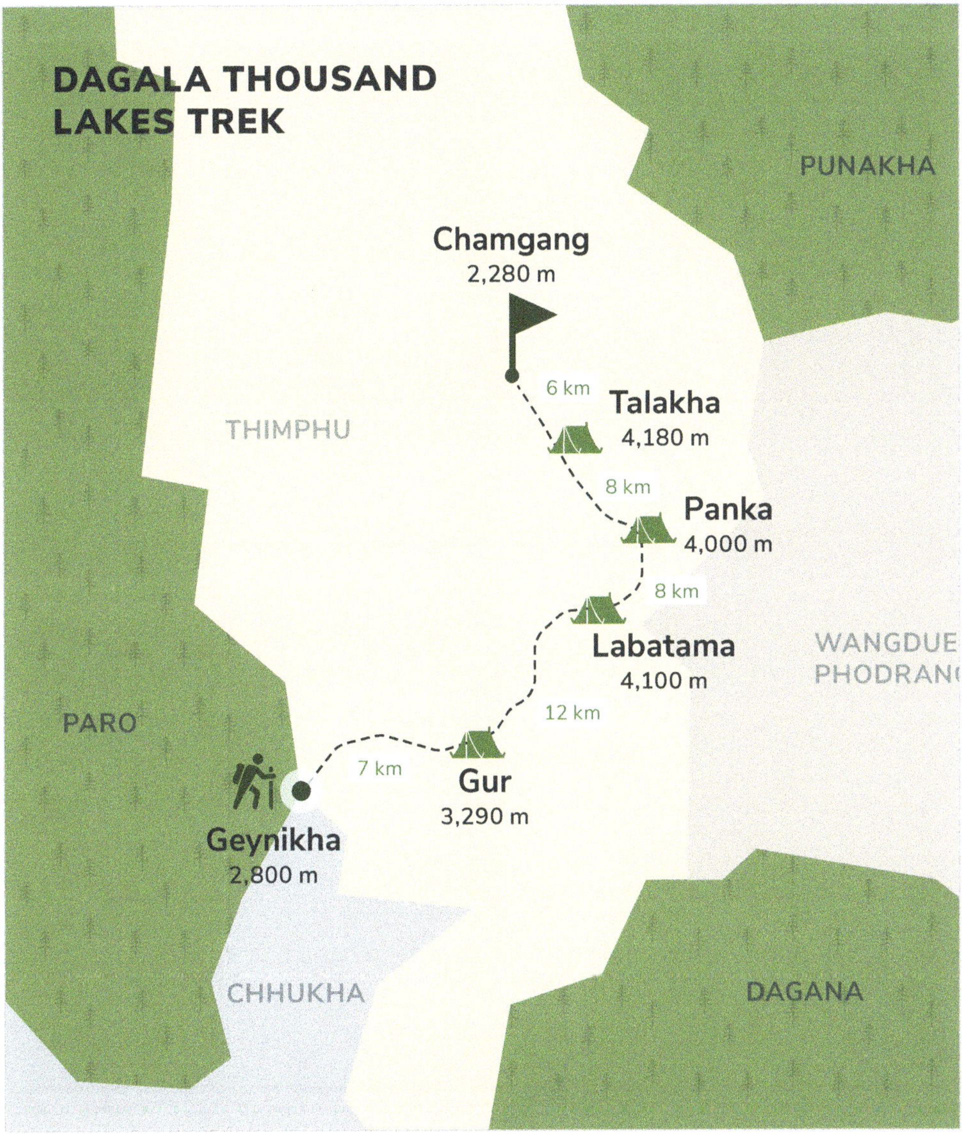

Highlights

- Hike through an ancient trail that was once an important trade route connecting Thimphu and Dagana
- Catch a sight of the breathtaking peaks of Mt Everest, Mt Jomolhari, and Mt Jichu Drake
- Hike through pristine alpine lakes, high yak pastures and beautiful meadows
- Traverse through mountain villages of Gur, Labatama, and Panka
- Experience the unique local semi-nomadic lifestyle
- Discover some of the most sacred Buddhist monasteries
- Visit the iconic Taktsang Monastery (Tiger's Nest Monastery)

Find out more

s.bn.sg/dagala

Dagala Thousand Lakes Trek takes you by many small beautiful lakes

Jomolhari Loop Trek

7 OR 11 DAYS

Difficulty level:	**Moderate to Difficult**
Max elevation:	**5,000 m**
Min elevation:	**2,500 m**
Season:	**March to October**
Start from:	**Sharna Zampa**
End at:	**Gunitsawa**

Magnificent view of the Himalayan mountains

Jomolhari Loop Trek, also known as Soi Yaksa Trek, is one of Bhutan's most popular medium-level treks. Do not confuse it with the extended main Jomolhari Trek. It's the perfect trek for avid hikers who want to soak up the diverse landscapes of Bhutan. The altitude of Jomolhari Loop Trek ranges from 2,500 m to around 5,000 m. You can expect to see a wide variety of flora and fauna. Embark on Jomolhari Loop Trek for a fantastic panoramic view of the majestic Mount Jomolhari.

A fairly high level of fitness is required to complete the trek.

Average	**High**	Ultra High

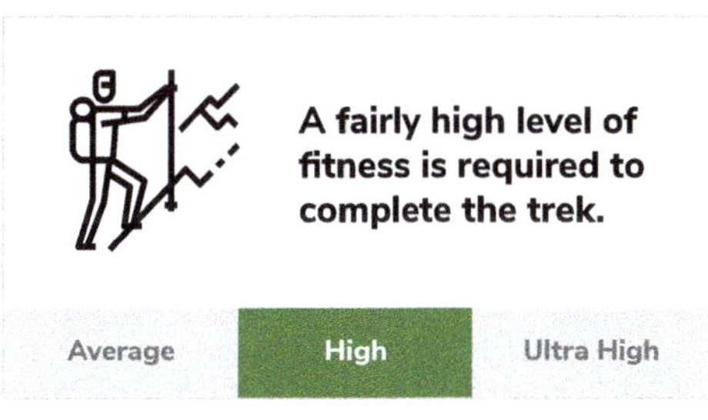

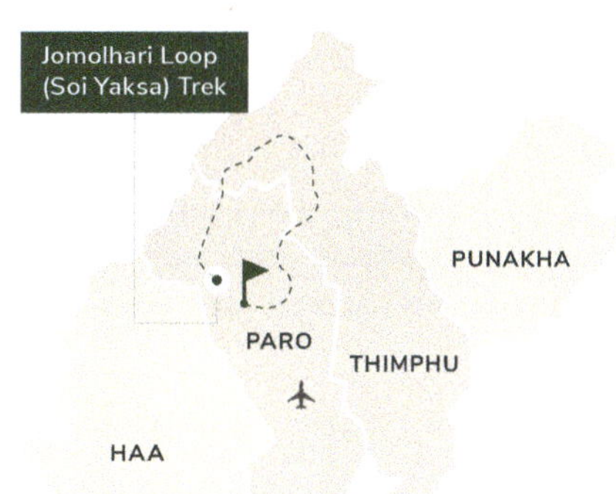

JOMOLHARI LOOP (SOI YAKSA) TREK

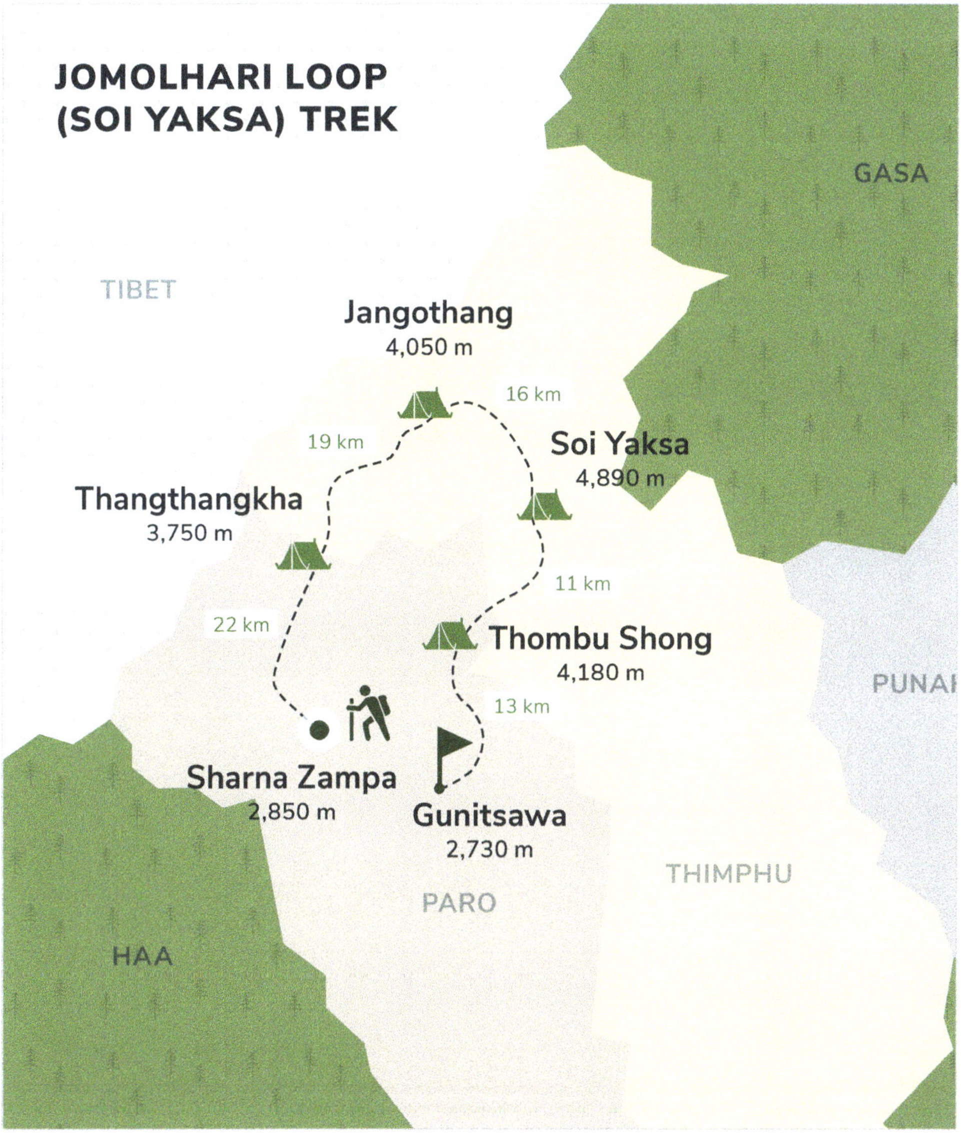

Highlights

- Experience astounding views of snow-capped mountains such as Mt Jomolhari and Mt Jichu Drake
- Traverse a variety of spectacular landscapes; enjoy the local flora and fauna
- Camp at the base of the sacred Mt Jomolhari
- Encounter wildlife such as blue sheep, marmots and the elusive snow leopards
- Discover Bhutan's unique culture with farmhouse visits
- Visit the iconic Taktsang Monastery (Tiger's Nest Monastery)

Find out more

s.bn.sg/jomol

Stunning scenery and night view from the campsite

Merak-Sakteng Trek

18 DAYS

Difficulty level:	**Moderate to Difficult**
Max elevation:	**4,100 m**
Min elevation:	**1,500 m**
Season:	**Mar to May, Sep to Nov**
Start from:	**Chaling**
End at:	**Phongmey**

The lush green valleys of eastern Bhutan

The Merak-Sakteng Trek will take you to explore the nomadic areas of Bhutan. Unlike in the past, a new farm road now connects Merak to Sakteng. The trek is for adventurous souls who would like to explore the remote far east regions of the country.

The exotic valleys of Merak and Sakteng have been home to the indigenous tribes, the Brokpas, for centuries since their displacement from Tibet. The distinctive customs and lifestyle of the Brokpas make Merak and Sakteng rewarding places to explore. You will see Brokpas in attires and homes made out of yak hair!

A fairly high level of fitness is required to complete the trek.

Average	High	Ultra High

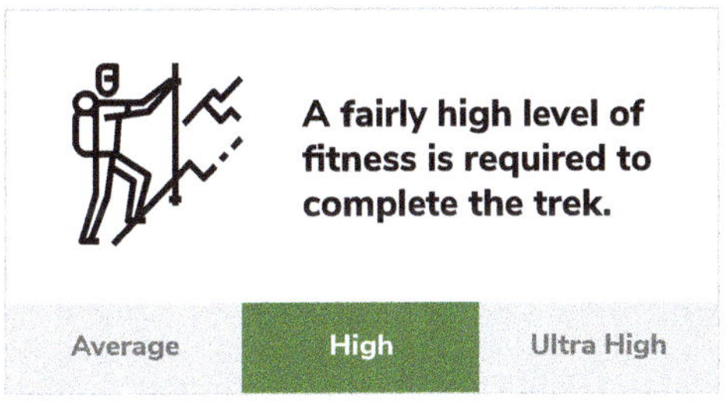

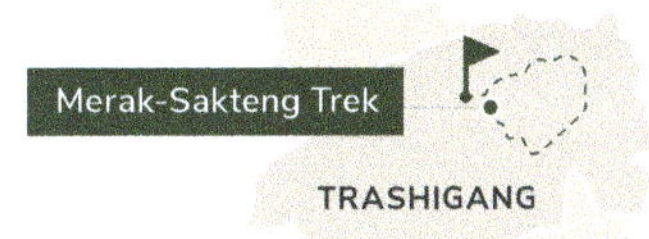

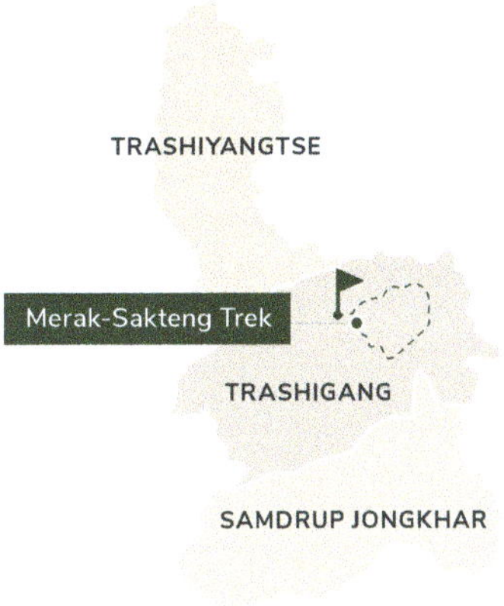

MERAK-SAKTENG TREK

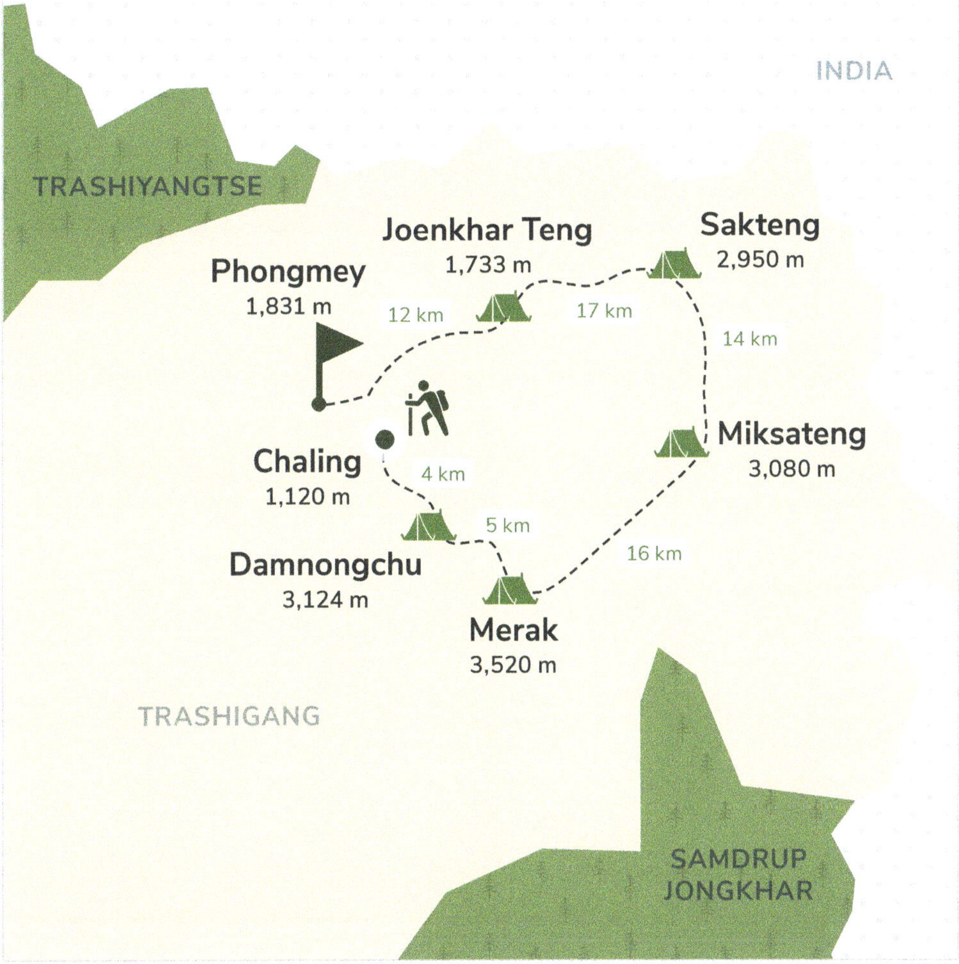

Highlights

- Explore the Sakteng Wildlife Sanctuary, home to endangered animals, as well as the elusive and mythical yetis — locally known as *migois*
- Immerse in the rich biodiversity of Bhutan
- Hike through the Bumthang district, the spiritual heartland of Bhutan
- Explore eastern Bhutan's most scenic, pastoral valleys and remote villages
- Experience the unique lifestyle, culture, and tradition of the Brokpas
- Visit the iconic Taktsang Monastery (Tiger's Nest Monastery)

Find out more

s.bn.sg/bttreks

Most of the highlanders in Bhutan are yak herders

Trans Bhutan Trail

Difficulty level:	**Moderate to Difficult**
Max elevation:	**4,100 m**
Min elevation:	**1,500 m**
Season:	**Mar to May, Sep to Nov**
Start from:	**Chaling**
End at:	**Phongmey**

37 DAYS

The lush green valleys of eastern Bhutan

For centuries, the Trans Bhutan Trail (TBT) served as a vital route for pilgrims, messengers, armies, and traders, representing the sole means of travel and communication across the country until the 1960s. Today, it has been rejuvenated for a new era of adventure and connectivity.

Embark on the ultimate trekking adventure in Bhutan by taking on the Trans Bhutan Trail end-to-end hike, renowned as one of the world's most extraordinary journeys. Covering 403 kilometers from Haa in the west to Trashigang in the east, this hike will lead you through a plethora of historical and religious sites, diverse climate zones,

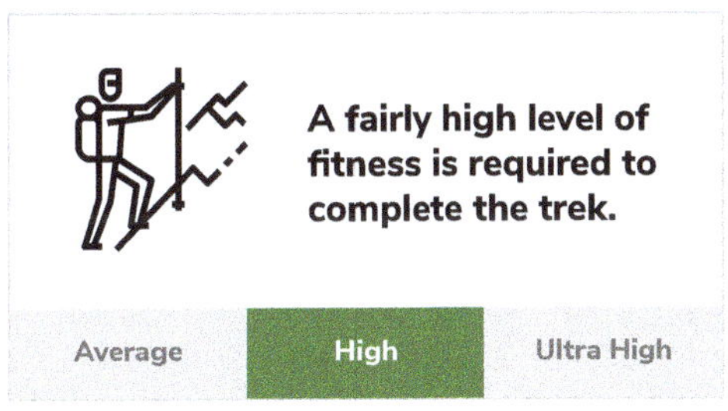

and immersive cultural experiences. Along the way, you'll have rest days scheduled in Punakha and Bumthang.

Accommodations on this journey include a mix of locally-owned 3* hotels and TBT Signature Campsites. TBT campsites feature semi-permanent tents, showers, toilets, hot stone baths (where available), and locally sourced organic dinner options. If you prefer a 4* or 5* upgrade, please inform your tour operator.

In 2018, under the wisdom and vision of His Majesty, The King, the Bhutan Canada Foundation, supported by the Department of Tourism, led the restoration of the Trail, making it accessible once again to locals, pilgrims, and travelers. During the COVID-19 crisis, with the assistance of the Royal Government of Bhutan, over 900 furloughed workers played a vital role in restoring the Trail to its former glory. This restoration effort included rebuilding 18 bridges, constructing hundreds of kilometers of footpaths, and creating over 10,000 steps. Today, the 403-kilometer Trail can be traversed by walking, running, or biking, either in part or as a whole.

The Trail includes stops at 27 Gewogs, 4 Dzongs, 21 temples, 12 mountain passes, 5 suspension bridges, 10 cantilever bridges, 77 chortens, and 30 stupas. It traverses a diverse range of landscapes, from vibrant rice paddies and lush rhododendron forests to dense wilderness, secluded villages, and lively towns. Furthermore, it passes through several of Bhutan's prominent urban centers, including Thimphu, the capital, and the royal city of Bumthang.

The difficulty level of the Trans Bhutan Trail can be tailored to your preferences. We provide a comprehensive 36-day End-to-End itinerary for those seeking the full experience, but the Trail is also divided into smaller, more manageable routes, allowing you to choose an option that suits your comfort and fitness level. Additionally, we offer an itinerary for those interested in running sections of the Trans Bhutan Trail.

In terms of altitude, the Trail generally maintains a moderate elevation, with the highest point ranging between 3,900 and 4,000 meters (12,795 and 13,123 feet) above sea level.

Highlights

- Embark on a remarkable journey spanning from the western town of Haa to the eastern enclave of Trashigang, covering the breadth of Bhutan's breathtaking landscapes
- Pass through a total of 26 counties, each offering its unique cultural, natural, and historical treasures, providing an in-depth glimpse into Bhutan's diversity.
- Admire the awe-inspiring architectural beauty of 4 Dzongs, which serve as both historical fortresses and vital administrative centers, showcasing Bhutan's rich heritage and tradition.
- Visit 21 temples, each steeped in spirituality and cultural significance, allowing you to immerse yourself in Bhutan's profound religious practices and heritage.
- Traverse 12 mountain passes, conquering rugged terrains and gaining access to spectacular panoramic views of Bhutan's majestic landscapes, including towering peaks and lush valleys.
- Walk across 5 suspension bridges and 10 cantilever bridges, adding an element of adventure to your journey as you cross roaring rivers and deep gorges, creating unforgettable memories.
- Circumambulate 77 chortens and 30 stupas, providing you with opportunities for spiritual reflection and connection with Bhutan's rich cultural heritage.

Find out more

s.bn.sg/bttreks

Traverse 12 mountain passes and conquering rugged terrains

Lunana Snowman Trek

28 DAYS

Difficulty level:	**Challenging**
Max elevation:	**5,320 m**
Min elevation:	**2,850 m**
Season:	**May to October**
Start from:	**Drukgyel Dzong**
End at:	**Sephu**

The indigenous Layaps in their traditional dress with their iconic conical hat

Snowman Trek is one of the most challenging treks in the world due to its high altitude, duration and distance, but it is also one of the most rewarding and beautiful treks in the Himalayas. The trail covers a distance of 230 km with an extreme elevation gain of 3,140 m. It goes through many steep ascents and descents.

Snowman Trek is the longest, remotest and undoubtedly most epic trek in the Himalayas. You will cross twelve mountain passes from 4,500 m to over 5,000 m. This demanding trek will bring you on a spectacular journey through Laya and Lunana. You'll encounter some of the world's rarest wildlife along the trek, such as the snow leopards.

Completing the Snowman Trek is truly an achievement to boast of as more people are climbing Mount Everest than those finishing the Snowman Trek!

An ultra high level of fitness and endurance is required to complete the trek.

Average	High	**Ultra High**

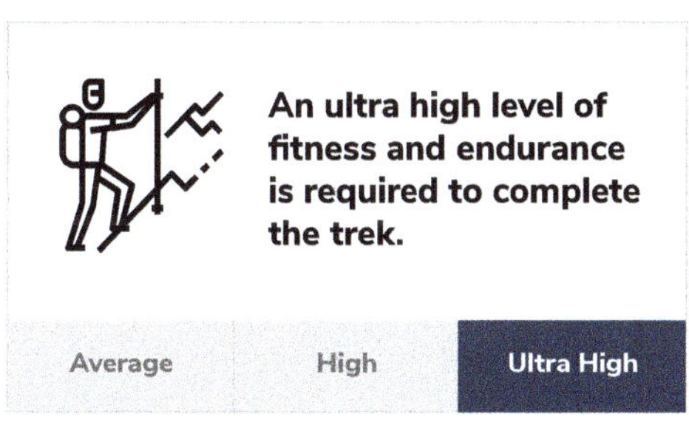

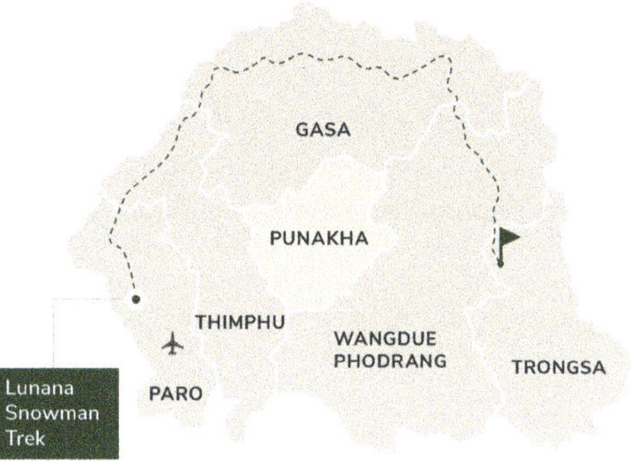

LUNANA SNOWMAN TREK

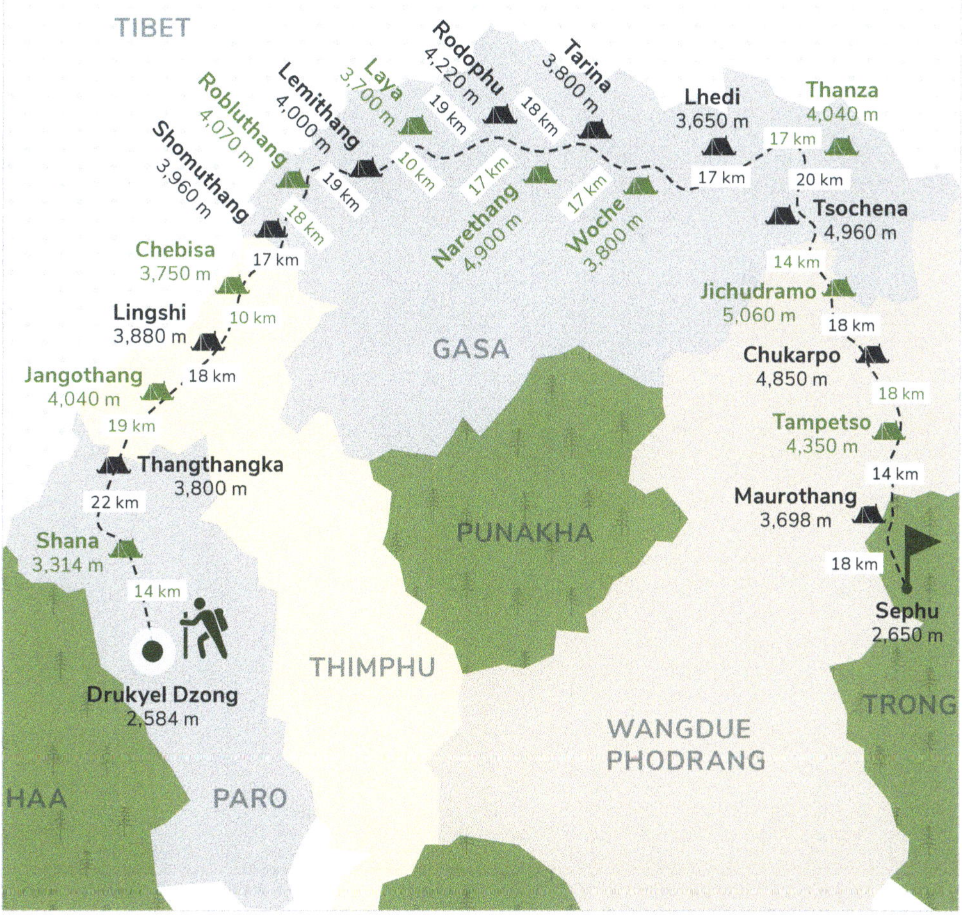

Highlights

- Cross twelve high mountain passes
- Explore the isolated Laya community and Bhutan's most remote region of Lunana
- Traverse beautiful landscapes, from lush valleys and dense forests to high mountain passes
- Get rewarded with spectacular views of Mt Jomolhari, Mt Jichu Drake, Masangang, Tiger Mountain, and Gangkar Puensum
- Soak in the Gasa Hot Springs to rejuvenate your body
- Explore and interact with the friendly yak herders
- Experience the unique cultures of the semi-nomadic tribes in Laya and Lunana
- Visit the iconic Taktsang Monastery (Tiger's Nest Monastery)

Fun fact

- An inaugural Snowman Run was held successfully on October 13, 2022.
- The course followed the Snowman Trekking Route and the participants in the The Snowman Race completed the run in just 5 days.

Find out more

s.bn.sg/snowman

You'll see Bhutanese women threshing wheat using flails

Admire the breathtaking views of the Himalayan mountains by embarking on a trek

Travel
Tips

Part of the thrill of travelling is in the planning. This section brings you essential travel tips and recommendations as you prepare for your journey to Bhutan.

Travelling to Bhutan

Travel by Air

There is currently only one international airport in Bhutan, and it's located in the Paro district. You can only book flights to Bhutan through the national airline, Royal Bhutan Airlines, known as Drukair, or the privately owned Tashi Airlines, known as Bhutan Airlines.

Drukair flies to Bhutan from:
- Bangkok (Thailand)
- Singapore
- Kathmandu (Nepal)
- Dhaka (Bangladesh)
- New Delhi, Kolkata, Gaya, Bagdogra, and Guwahati (India)
- Dubai (UAE)

Bhutan Airlines flies to Bhutan from:
- Bangkok (Thailand)
- Kathmandu (Nepal)
- Delhi and Kolkata (India)

Paro Airport has an extremely narrow runway

If you are planning to travel to Bhutan, you are required to apply for a tourist visa. Check out **www.visit.doi.gov.bt** for more information on the e-visa application. If you are booking through a tour operator, they will be able to process it for you.

Book your trip **at least four to six months in advance**, especially if you plan to travel during the peak seasons of spring (February to May) or autumn (September to November). There are limited scheduled flights, and flights are restricted to daylight hours due to the difficulties in navigating the terrains. Hence, you should avoid a tight connecting flight.

Paro International Airport

With mountains as high as 5,000 m surrounding the airport and a narrow landing strip that is 2,265 m long and visible only moments before landing, it is no surprise that Paro Airport is deemed one of the most dangerous airports to land in. Other airports rely on the ILS (Instrument Landing System) to guide the aircraft laterally and vertically in an approach to land.

On the other hand, the pilots only have one VOR (Very high-frequency Omni-directional Range) to guide them at Paro Airport. Most airports offer at least 18 km (10 nautical miles) of distance for pilots to gauge an aligned approach onto the landing strip, but Paro Airport accords only 1.8 km to 3.7 km (one to two nautical miles). All the factors above demand for the pilots to be very precise in landing. Thus only a handful of highly experienced pilots are qualified to land in Paro Airport.

Check out **www.paroairport.com** for the latest flight schedules.

When your trip is confirmed, your tour operator will arrange for your tour guide to receive you at the airport.

If you have limited time in Bhutan, you can consider taking a domestic flight to reduce travel time. There are three domestic airports in Bhutan:

- Bathpalathang Airport (Bumthang)
- Gelephu Airport (Sarpang)
- Yonphulla Aiport (Trashigang)

Spectacular Himalayan mountains surround the Paro Airport

Travel by Land

You can also travel to Bhutan by land through the border towns via Phuentsholing, Samdrup Jongkhar or Gelephu.

Phuentsholing is located in southern Bhutan and is connected to the town of Jaigaon in India. It will take approximately six hours to drive 180 km from Phuentsholing to Bhutan's capital, Thimphu.

You can also enter via land from Samdrup Jongkhar in eastern Bhutan through the state of Assam in India. The journey from Guwahati Airport in India will take about three hours to reach Samdrup Jongkhar. Travellers usually enter through the Samdrup Jongkhar gateway if they intend to explore the districts in eastern Bhutan such as Trashigang, Trashiyangtse, Mongar or Lhuentse.

Gelephu, another land entry point bordering the state of West Bengal in India, features a modern and integrated checkpost for smoother border formalities. From here, you will need to travel across three districts —Sarpang, Tsirang, Wangdue Phodrang— to reach Thimphu, with a journey time of approximately ten hours.

Drukair at the runway of Paro Airport with the magnificent Paro Dzong in the background

Keep a lookout for all the tongue-in-cheek road signs in Bhutan

Bring along your medications if you are prone to motion sickness as the roads can be very winding

When should you visit Bhutan?

> Aside from the weather patterns, something to consider when planning a trip to Bhutan is the festival schedule. Festivals are great opportunties to immerse in the local culture.

Spring (Mar - May)

Spring is the popular season for tourists to visit Bhutan as the weather is ideal, and it's an excellent time for trekking. The valleys are green and lush as spring brings new growth with rhododendron, wild azaleas and wildflowers blooming from March to May.

Spring recommendations:
- Paro Tshechu in Paro (early April)
- Gomkora Festival in Trashigang (April)
- Savour the beautiful jacaranda blossoms at Punakha Dzong (April and May)
- Jomolhari Trek & Bumdra Trek (mid-April till end-May)

We highly recommend that you book your trip in advance. Flight tickets and hotels for the spring season are usually fully booked as early as January.

Experience the vibrant sacred dances of Bhutan

Paro Tshechu

Paro Tshechu is the most popular religious festival in Bhutan. This significant festival has been held annually since the 17th century when Zhabdrung Ngawang Namgyel and Ponpo Rigzin Nyingpo initiated the festival in conjunction with the consecration of Paro Dzong in 1644. Paro Tshechu is held for five days, and attending one will give you a great understanding of Bhutan's rich culture and history.

Check out
Paro Tshechu

s.bn.sg/parofest

Each dance performance has a story or special meaning behind it

The sacred Black Hat Dance where monks subdue demons with their spinning trance performance

Summer (Jun - Aug)

Although monsoon season starts in June and continues until August, Bhutan usually experiences only light showers in the afternoon. Occasionally, some drizzles last the entire day. Summer is the best time to visit Bhutan if you would like a closer and clearer view of the Himalayan mountains and to indulge in the lush green paddy fields. With lesser crowds during the summer, you can better soak in the atmosphere at the different attractions. With the days being longer in summer, you will also get to explore more places than you would during other seasons.

Summer recommendations:

- Nimalung Tshechu in Bumthang (June)
- Kurjey Tshechu in Bumthang (June)
- Masutake Mushroom Festival in Thimphu (August)

Nimalung Tshechu

Nimalung Tshechu is a 3-day festival held in Nimalung Buddhist Monastery in central Bhutan. It begins with the usual Cham performances. On the final day, visitors are blessed with the display of Guru Tshengye *thongdrel*.

The sound of the drums symbolises that Buddhism itself has no visible form

Drametse Ngacham is a sacred masked dance of the drums that originated from eastern Bhutan 500 years ago

Autumn (Sep - Nov)

Just like spring, autumn is also a peak season for Bhutan due to the pleasantly mild weather with clear and crisp blue skies. It is one of the best times for trekking too as the climate is cool and temperate. You may look forward to basking in rice fields as they turn gold before the harvest.

Autumn recommendations:
- Thimphu Tshechu in Thimphu (September)
- Jakar Tshechu in Bumthang (October)
- Jambay Lhakhang Drup & Prakar Tshechu in Bumthang (November)
- Black-necked Crane Festival in Phobjikha Valley (11 November)

Thimphu Tshechu

The 3-day festival gathers the largest audience of all the festivals in Bhutan. The tshechu is preceded by days and nights of prayers and rituals to invoke the gods. Monks prepare themselves with meditation and prayer for weeks ahead of the festival. The carnival-like atmosphere is a great opportunity for you to learn about Bhutan's rich cultural traditions.

A play that depicts the Buddhist philosophy that everything is impermanent

The Black Hat Dance represents the tantric ritual of slaying the unruly demonic forces

Winter (Dec - Feb)

Winter is the best time for an exclusive experience on a snowy landscape in Bhutan. The weather can be cold in December, but the lowest temperature often occurs near the end of January.

The higher regions usually experience snowfall. Heavy snowfall may cause some of the roads to central or eastern Bhutan to be impassable. If you would like to experience a less crowded Bhutan, winter is the time to visit as there are fewer tourists during this season. If you are lucky, you might even experience snowfall during your hike up to Taktsang Monastery (Tiger's Nest Monastery).

Winter recommendations:
- Druk Wangyel Tshechu (13 December)
- Bhutan's National Day (17 December)
- Trongsa Tshechu (December)
- Punakha Dromche & Tshechu (February)

Druk Wangyel Tshechu

Druk Wangyel Tshechu, established in 2011, is a special festival held as a tribute to the wise leadership of the fourth King, Jigme Singye Wangchuck and the armed forces' victory against the Assamese insurgents. Unlike the other festivals, the Royal Bhutan Army performs the dances during the festival instead of monks or commoners.

Check out Druk Wangyel Tshechu

s.bn.sg/dochulafest

The performances at Druk Wangyel Tshechu differ from the other tshechu festivals

One of the dances depicts five old men and women bestowing longevity and prosperity on the audience

Dancers portray celestial beings who bless and wish benefit upon all those in attendance

How much does it cost to travel to Bhutan?

Bhutan adheres to a 'High value, Low volume' tourism policy to avoid the effects of mass tourism. In the past, the government has implemented an all-inclusive tour package for all tourists visiting the country. Visitors were also required to book their trip through a licensed tour operator.

The restrictions were abolished on September 2022 and tourists are now able to explore Bhutan without going through a tour operator. However, booking an all inclusive trip from a reputable tour operator is still the most efficient way of getting the most out of your once-in-a-lifetime trip!

As of September 2023, all tourists except for India passport holders are required to pay a Sustainable Development Fees of USD100 per person per night. The levy will be in effect until September 2027.

The average cost of an all-inclusive package* to Bhutan is approximately USD 2150 for a 7D6N trip (excluding flight tickets).

Why should you still book a trip to Bhutan through a tour operator?

Local Expertise

Tour operators in Bhutan have extensive knowledge of the country, its culture, and its attractions. Experienced guides can provide valuable insights and recommendations that can enhance your trip. They are well-versed in local customs, traditions, and etiquette, ensuring that you have a respectful and culturally enriching experience.

Convenience

Planning a trip to Bhutan can be complex and time-consuming, especially when dealing with logistics like permits, accommodations, and transportation. Tour packages simplify this process by handling all the arrangements, allowing you to focus on enjoying your trip rather than worrying about the details.

Access to Restricted Areas

Some parts of Bhutan are restricted, and tourists can only visit them with a licensed tour operator. Booking a tour package ensures that you have access to these restricted areas, where you can explore unique cultural and natural treasures.

Cultural Immersion

Tour packages often include opportunities to participate in local festivals, visit monasteries, and interact with Bhutanese people. This cultural immersion can be a highlight of your trip and is often facilitated by tour operators.

Safety and Support

In the event of any unforeseen circumstances or emergencies, tour operators can provide support and assistance. They have local contacts and resources to ensure your safety and well-being during your trip.

The tour guides in Bhutan are knowledgeable and extremely friendly, don't hesitate to ask them questions

Do children have to pay the SDF?

Children aged 5 and below are exempted from the SDF. However, the visa application fee of USD40 is still applicable. Children aged 6 to 11 years old are only required to pay 50% of the SDF cost.

How much is the visa application fee?

The visa application fee costs USD40. It will take approximately 5 days to process your visa application. Check out **www.visit.doi.gov.bt** for more information. If you are booking a trip through a tour operator, they will be able to apply a visa on your behalf.

An all-inclusive package* typically covers the following costs and services:

- All internal taxes and charges
- Sustainable Development Fee (SDF) used by the government to provide free education, health care and to build infrastructures
- 3 meals a day
- A licensed English-speaking Bhutanese tour guide
- All transport on the ground including driver (excluding internal flights)
- A minimum 3-star accommodation (4-star & 5-star hotels will require an additional premium)
- Entrance fees to tourist attractions
- Camping equipment and haulage for trekking tours (if applicable)

Accommodation recommendations

Bhutan has strict rules and regulations for hotel management within the country. The Department of Tourism evaluates each hotel to ensure that the properties meet the standard and criteria required. Only those with a 3-star rating and above can host international tourists. Hence, as a tourist, you can have a peace of mind that your accommodations in Bhutan will be satisfying and comfortable.

If you book your trip to Bhutan through a tour operator, an all-inclusive tour package will include a standard 3-star accommodation. If you would like to upgrade to a 4-star or 5-star accommodation, there will be an additional cost depending on the hotel or resort that you choose.

Popular Standard Tourist Hotels

Paro
Lhahyuel Resort
Rema Resort
Silver Cloud Hotel
Zhideychen Resort

Thimphu
Hotel Changangkha
Khang Residency
Thimphu Central Hotel

Punakha
Dharma Siddhi
Meri Puensum Resort
Zhingkham Resort

Gangtey
ABC Lodge
Dewachen Hotel
Hotel Phobjikha
Phuentsho Yangkhil Resort

Bumthang
Dekyil Guest House
Swiss Guest House

Mongar
Wangchuk Hotel

Trashigang
Druk Deothjung Hotel

Top Luxury Hotels

Dawa at Hilltop by Heeton
Locations: Paro

Perched tranquilly on the slopes above Paro, Dawa at Hilltop by Heeton is a modern homage to Bhutan's soulful charm. The name Dawa, meaning "moon" in Dzongkha, reflects the resort's philosophy — to evoke serenity, clarity, and a sense of celestial escape.

Here, modern architecture harmonises with timeless Bhutanese aesthetics, crafting a sanctuary for those seeking beauty, peace, and connection. With 71 Deluxe Rooms, 15 Premium Rooms, and a singular Dawa Suite, each space is designed to immerse you in the surrounding landscape.

At Cypress – Fusion Restaurant, local ingredients are reimagined with global flair, while The D Bar invites you into an intimate setting for conversation, quiet moments, or after-dinner repose. Wellness is woven into every experience. The Chelela Spa offers rejuvenating rituals, the infinity-edge pool seems to merge with the mountain air, and the mountain-facing fitness studio keeps body and spirit in harmony.

From sunrise to starlight, Dawa at Hilltop is a place to slow down. Ancient monasteries, lush pine forests, and prayer flags all lie within reach.

Dawa at Hilltop Deluxe Valley View Room

COMO Uma Paro
Location: Paro

COMO Uma Paro is an exceptional choice for travellers seeking a deluxe stay that beautifully weaves Bhutanese tradition with contemporary elegance. Set amidst the pine-covered hills of the Paro Valley, this serene retreat captures the soul of Bhutan—peaceful, grounded, and deeply spiritual, while offering all the comforts of modern luxury.

As part of the world-renowned COMO Hotels and Resorts, COMO Uma Paro is celebrated for its refined aesthetics and warm, personalised service. Each room is a work of art, blending handcrafted Bhutanese craftsmanship— polished woodwork, intricate detailing, and vibrant handwoven fabrics—with the brand's signature minimalist design.

In 2008, the hotel gained worldwide attention when Hong Kong superstars Tony Leung and Carina Lau chose it for their wedding celebration, affirming its place among Bhutan's most exclusive sanctuaries.

Guests can savour fine Himalayan-inspired cuisine at the Bukhari restaurant, a royal favourite that highlights locally sourced ingredients and soulful flavours. COMO Uma Paro is a sanctuary for reflection—where stillness meets sophistication, and every sunrise over the valley feels like a quiet blessing.

COMO Uma Paro One Bedroom Villa

COMO Uma Punakha

Location: Punakha

COMO Uma Punakha, on the other hand, offers a more intimate yet equally luxurious retreat, perfectly suited for travellers seeking tranquillity and soul-deep renewal.

Perched at the western edge of the Punakha Valley, this secluded haven overlooks a sweeping, snake-like bend of the Mo Chhu River, where mist drifts over emerald hills and time seems to slow.

Consistently celebrated for its timeless excellence, COMO Uma Punakha has earned numerous prestigious accolades, including **Bhutan's Leading Hotel at the World Travel Awards (2018–2023), #3 Best Resort in Asia (2019) and Best Resort in Bhutan (2017)** by Condé Nast Traveler, and recognition among the **Top 20 Destination Spa Resorts in the World (2024).**

The lodge's design echoes the peace of its natural surroundings—sunlit interiors framed with intricate Bhutanese wood carvings and handwoven textiles create a feeling of harmony, warmth, and quiet elegance.

Guests can rejuvenate body and spirit with holistic therapies at Shambhala Retreat, then savour nourishing, farm-to-table cuisine crafted from the valley's freshest produce.

COMO Uma Punakha Valley View Room

Perched high above the pristine Paro Valley, Taj Paro Resort & Spa is where Bhutan's timeless spirit meets contemporary elegance. Every element of its architecture tells a story of sustainability crafted from locally sourced stone, reclaimed timber, and traditional Bhutanese techniques that honour the land.

This high-altitude sanctuary gazes across forest-clad hills and sacred Himalayan peaks, offering breath-taking, uninterrupted views of the legendary Paro Taktsang rising like a vision from the cliffs. Inside, 45 thoughtfully designed rooms and suites open to sweeping valley vistas, seamlessly blending modern comfort with artisanal heritage. Dining celebrates the rich bounty of Himalayan produce, while wellness spaces invite you to reconnect through J Wellness Circle therapies, meditation, and cultural rituals.

A traditional Bhutanese hot stone bath experience awaits, offering deep relaxation and healing amidst serene mountain surroundings.

From rainwater harvesting to energy-efficient design, every detail reflects a deep respect for Bhutan's sacred landscapes—creating a retreat where luxury feels natural and sustainability feels effortless. Taj's legendary hospitality makes every stay seamless and personal.

Taj Paro Resort & Spa Luxury Room with Tiger's Nest View

In the quiet embrace of Bhutan's Phobjikha Valley, Taj Gangtey Resort & Spa stands as a sanctuary where time slows and nature leads. Sustainability is woven into every aspect of its architectural design.

Cradled by forested ridges and sweeping alpine meadows, the resort's 35 mindfully curated rooms and suites open onto breath-taking views of the valley—a winter haven for the revered black-necked cranes, symbols of longevity and harmony.

Ideal for intimate gatherings and wellness retreats, Taj Gangtey offers handcrafted experiences: soul-nourishing cuisine sourced from Himalayan farms, and nature-integrated therapies at the J Wellness Circle Spa.

Experience the traditional Bhutanese hot stone bath, a soothing ritual that combines mineral-rich river stones and healing herbs to restore balance and vitality. Stargazing decks invite you to witness the vast Himalayan sky in its purest form, a humbling reminder of stillness and simplicity.

Taj Gangtey is a stay that lingers long after you leave like a crane's call in the morning mist — gentle yet unforgettable.

Taj Gangtey Resort & Spa Grand Luxury Suite

Zhiwaling Heritage

Locations: Paro

Set amidst a garden of flowers and trees in the Paro Valley, Zhiwaling Heritage stands as a testament to Bhutanese craftsmanship and hospitality. Blending timeless artistry with contemporary comfort, the property feels like a living museum where Bhutanese culture is not merely showcased but genuinely experienced by its guests.

Hand-carved woodwork, finely laid stone masonry, and exquisitely hand-painted motifs define its architecture, each detail meticulously crafted by skilled Bhutanese artisans using time-honoured techniques.

The Junior Suites offer generous space and sweeping valley views, while the One-Bedroom Suites provide serene retreats and private sanctuaries adorned with intricate details and light interiors.

For added exclusivity, the Royal Raven Suite features elegant interiors, panoramic views, and a private shrine, perfect for special occasions or extended stays.

Charming cottage-style accommodations lend Zhiwaling Heritage a warm, village-like atmosphere that invites exploration and reflection. A temple reconstructed with 450-year-old timber from Gangtey Monastery connects the property to Bhutan's spiritual

Zhiwaling Heritage Raven Suite Room

heritage. Meandering paths lead to flower-filled courtyards, traditional hot-stone baths offering deep relaxation, and dining that celebrates seasonal Bhutanese ingredients alongside international favourites at the Pizza Patio.

At the Soe-Thab & Gallery, guests can join butter tea ceremonies, explore Bhutanese culinary traditions, or enjoy a ceramic painting session led by the resident artisan.

Wellness is seamlessly integrated into the Zhiwaling experience, from guided meditation and yoga sessions to a tranquil spa offering therapies inspired by Himalayan botanicals. Beyond the hotel, the surrounding valleys invite peaceful leisurely walks.

Above all, it is the warmth of Zhiwaling's team that defines the stay. Many have been with the hotel since its opening in 2005, embodying the essence of genuine Bhutanese hospitality.

The hotel has also earned international acclaim for its cultural integrity and sustainable ethos, becoming the first and only Bhutanese property recognised by National Geographic's Unique Lodges of the World and receiving multiple South Asian Travel Awards for Leading Heritage Hotel and Leading Eco-Friendly Resort.

Zhiwaling Heritage is the only 5-star hotel in Bhutan wholly and proudly owned by Bhutanese

Nestled in the heart of Bhutan's capital, Pemako Thimphu rises like a modern fortress of tranquillity. Inspired by dzong architecture, its majestic form mirrors Bhutan's ancient strongholds, grounding guests in timeless heritage even as the city stirs around it.

Inside, 66 elegantly appointed rooms and suites adorned with traditional art and hand-painted murals offer a sanctuary of calm. From cosy nooks overlooking the city to terraces that open to Himalayan vistas, every space invites quiet reflection and repose.

Culinary journeys here blend Bhutanese soul with worldly flair. Chig Ja Gye reimagines traditional flavours with authenticity and finesse, while The Thongsel enchants with its refined design, gentle fountains, and the meditative rhythm of prayer wheels.

After dusk, the intimate Ara Bar beckons with handcrafted cocktails and moments of stillness.

Wellness at Pemako is both restorative and spiritual. The Lotus Realm Spa draws from Sowa-Rigpa healing traditions, complemented by a heated indoor pool, steam rooms, and serene movement spaces.

Pemako Thimphu Deluxe Room

Pemako Punakha
Location: Punakha

Conceptualised by acclaimed designer Bill Bensley, Pemako Punakha is cradled in the fertile heart of the Punakha Valley and embraced by the gentle flow of the Mochu River. Inspired by the mythical *beyul*, the hidden valleys of enlightenment — this luxurious tented retreat is an earthly paradise waiting to be discovered.

Each villa is a private cocoon of serenity, blending Bhutanese craftsmanship with modern sophistication. Spacious decks open to sweeping valley views, while private heated pools invite unhurried rest. Interiors feature handwoven Bhutanese textiles, copper accents, and refined materials like Serge Ferrari fabrics. Achemy House revives Bhutanese heritage recipes in a restored traditional setting, Soma serves comforting global dishes, and Sura curates intimate dining under the stars. The Lotus Realm Spa restores balance through Sowa-Rigpa, Bhutan's ancient healing tradition.

Amongst its many accolades are Condé Nast Traveler's Best New Hotels in the World 2024, Robb Report's 50 Greatest Luxury Hotels on Earth 2024, and Readers' Choice Awards 2025 – Runner-up, 'Rest of Asia'. Pemako is where peace finds you, wonder surrounds you, and time gently slows down.

Pemako Punakha Luxury Tented Pool Villa

Amankora

The first resort in Bhutan with five lodges across its central and western valleys, Amankora has been part of this legendary Buddhist kingdom for 17 years. Amankora's five lodges are sanctuaries designed to complement its uniquely beautiful setting. Aman is one of the iconic brands to have emerged from Asia, dedicated to providing an unparalleled experience.

Widely acclaimed as one of the best luxury resort brands globally, Aman is known for premium service and luxury, high-profile clientele and the most exotic locations. 'Aman' means 'peace' in Sanskrit, and 'kora' means 'circumambulate' in Dzongkha.

In recognition of its exceptional standards of hospitality, Amankora has been awarded **Two MICHELIN Keys,** a testament to its refined design, serene atmosphere, and impeccable service. Surrounded by forests and orchards, the five lodges comprise 76 suites that fuse rustic elements with contemporary design.

There is no television in the rooms, though you probably don't need it given the stunning views surrounding the lodges. Each lodge organises different activities in the evening. You can enjoy cultural programmes with traditional Bhutanese dances at the Thimphu and Punakha lodges.

Amankora Punakha Suite

Six Senses

Six Senses is a luxury brand renowned for its focus on wellness and sustainability. The five Six Senses Bhutan lodges have been thoughtfully designed to fully immerse travellers in the kingdom's natural beauty and culture, offering a contemporary take on traditional Bhutanese architecture and form. The lodges, which vary in style from valley to valley, showcase each location's diversity and special character.

The properties range in size and facilities, but all of Six Senses' properties are focused on sustainability practices, echoing the values of Bhutan. In recognition of its exceptional commitment to sustainability, design, and guest experience, Six Senses Bhutan has been awarded **One MICHELIN Key**, marking a proud milestone as one of the most distinguished hospitality brands in the Kingdom.

Six Senses Punakha, also known as 'The Flying Farmhouse Amidst the Rice Fields', is the most popular lodge. This spectacular lodge has a more rustic rural feel, complementing the warmer climate it's in while offering sweeping views of the valley filled with rice paddy fields and dotted with traditional farmhouses. A highlight of Six Senses Punakha is the crescent-shaped outdoor infinity pool overlooking the stunning Punakha valley.

Six Senses Paro Lodge Suite

&BEYOND Punakha River Lodge
Location: Punakha

&BEYOND Punakha River Lodge, nestled deep within the lush green Punakha Valley and positioned along the banks of the Mo Chu river, is a remarkable retreat.

Currently, it offers six cozy luxury tents, a one-bedroom suite known as the River House, and a two-bedroom suite referred to as the Family Suite. The lodge is surrounded by vast stretches of vibrant rice paddies and dense clusters of forested hills.

Crafted with intricate detail, the lodge embodies traditional Bhutanese architectural style and seamlessly blends into its natural surroundings. This marks &BEYOND's inaugural lodge in the splendid kingdom of Bhutan.

For those seeking relaxation, the lodge offers a selection of soothing treatments and wellness therapies, set amidst the serene surroundings of the spa, which is situated in an orange orchard near a tranquil perennial stream.

You can harmonize your chakras with gentle yoga sessions or luxuriate in a traditional Bhutanese hot stone bath, a must-try experience.

&BEYOND Punakha River Lodge Tented Suite

Gangtey Lodge
Locations: Gangtey

Gangtey Lodge is an intimate hideaway set on a gentle hillside above the valley overlooking the mystical Phobjikha Valley, winter home to the endangered black-necked cranes. Inspired by Bhutanese vernacular architecture, it blends rustic charm with understated luxury, offering travellers a serene sanctuary that captures the true spirit of Bhutan.

Every corner of the lodge feels warm and inviting, from the flickering fireplace in the main lounge to the deep, freestanding tubs in each suite, perfectly positioned to frame sweeping valley views.

Beyond its elegant design, Gangtey Lodge is deeply rooted in community and sustainability, supporting local initiatives and employing villagers from the surrounding area.

Guests are invited to slow down, connect with nature, and experience authentic Bhutanese hospitality through spiritual blessings, gentle hikes, and heartfelt interactions with locals.

In recognition of its exceptional service, refined design, and soulful connection to its surroundings, Gangtey Lodge Bhutan has been awarded Two MICHELIN Keys, affirming its reputation as one of the Kingdom's most exceptional and heartfelt retreats.

Gangtey Lodge Suite

Bhutan Spirit Sanctuary
Location: Paro

Himalayan Keys Forest Paro
Location: Paro, Thimphu

Le Méridien
Location: Paro, Thimphu

Naksel Boutique
Location: Paro

Rustic Roots Resort
Location: Paro

Terma Linca Resort
Location: Thimphu

Mani Ratna Resort
Location: Thimphu

Norkhil Boutique Hotel
Location: Thimphu

Thimphu Capitol
Location: Thimphu

The Pema by Realm
Location: Thimphu

The Postcard Dewa
Location: Thimphu

Zhiwa Ling Ascent
Location: Thimphu

Yarkay, Thimphu-IHCL SeleQtions
Location: Thimphu

Dhensa Boutique Resort
Location: Punakha

Lobesa Boutique Hotel
Location: Punakha

Dharma Siddhi is a boutique homestay offering luxurious comfort amidst the serene beauty of Punakha

Rimphu Heritage
Location: Paro

Paro Village View Homestay
Location: Paro

Travellers Village Homestay
Location: Paro

Kinley Om Homestay
Location: Thimphu

Mendrelgang Homestay
Location: Punakha

Lala Homestay
Location: Punakha

Chimi Lhakhang Village
Location: Punakha

Aum Dechen Om Homestay
Location: Punakha

Lhakpa Homestay
Location: Gangtey

Karma Wangmo Homestay
Location: Gangtey

Kumbu Lhamo Homestay
Location: Gangtey

Passang Zam Homestay
Location: Gangtey

Pem Village Homestay
Location: Gangtey

Soednam Zingkha Heritage
Locations: Haa

Ngawang Homestay
Location: Bumthang

Rimphu Heritage is a historic homestay blending Bhutanese tradition, family legends, and modern comforts

Climate and Temperature

The climate in Bhutan varies due to its topography and differences in altitudes. Bhutan has three climatic zones: subtropical in the south, temperate in the middle and subalpine in the north.

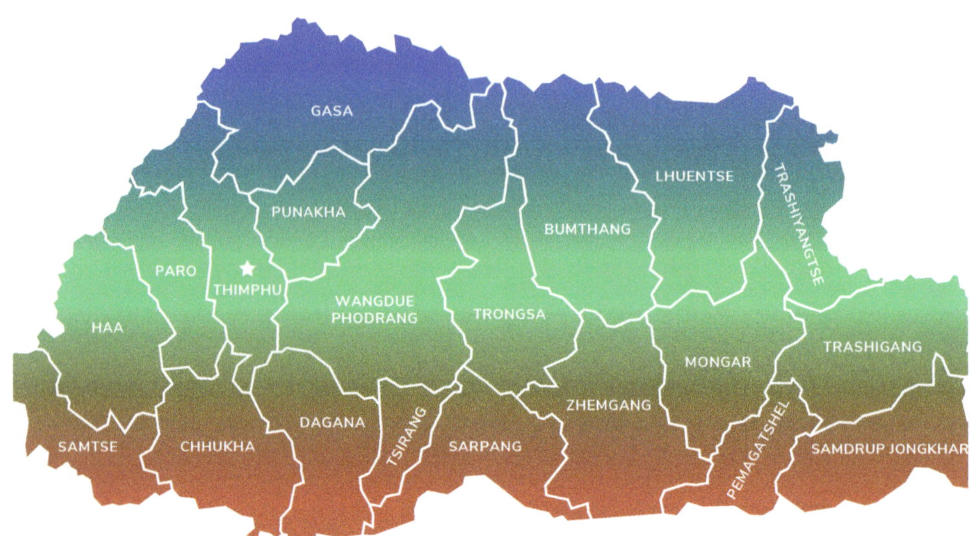

Climatic Zones of Bhutan

Northern Zone

The northern zone has a harsher climate and is much colder during winter. Mountain peaks are perpetually covered in snow, and lower-lying areas are cool in summer.

Central Zone

The central zone has a seasonal climate with warm summers before the monsoon. The winters are usually cool and dry with clear blue skies.

Cold climate in northern Bhutan

Clear blue skies in central Bhutan

Temp in	°c	Jan	Feb	Mar	Apr	May	Jun	Jul	Aug	Sep	Oct	Nov	Dec
Paro west	max	9.4	13.4	14.5	17.6	23.5	25.4	26.8	25.3	23.4	18.7	13.9	11.2
	min	-5.8	1.5	0.6	4.6	10.6	13.1	14.9	14.7	11.7	7.4	1.4	-1.7
Thimphu west	max	12.3	14.4	16.4	20.0	22.5	24.4	18.9	25.0	23.1	19.1	17.9	14.5
	min	-2.6	0.6	3.9	7.1	13.1	15.2	13.4	15.8	15.0	10.4	0.5	-1.1
Punakha west	max	16.1	19.6	21.2	24.4	27.2	31.2	32.0	31.4	29.9	27.8	22.3	15.0
	min	4.2	5.3	9.2	11.9	14.8	19.5	21.6	19.8	20.0	18.9	13.0	7.9
Wangdue west	max	17.0	19.0	22.8	26.2	29.9	29.2	18.4	29.1	27.5	26.1	22.6	19.1
	min	4.3	7.8	10.4	12.9	17.7	20.1	16.2	20.0	19.1	14.7	9.6	6.3
Trongsa central	max	13.0	13.9	16.7	20.1	21.0	22.2	25.3	23.8	22.6	21.8	19.8	18.2
	min	-0.2	0.4	4.4	6.6	11.6	13.6	15.3	15.0	14.2	11.7	6.4	2.5
Bumthang central	max	10.8	10.0	16.2	18.7	21.3	22.5	14.1	23.0	21.6	19.5	16.1	12.3
	min	-5.1	-1.4	3.5	3.9	9.5	13.5	10.9	13.7	12.1	5.9	-0.5	-2.3
Mongar east	max	15.5	15.9	20.0	22.8	25.1	26.1	27.1	25.4	24.7	22.7	19.9	17.7
	min	8.2	8.3	11.6	14.0	17.4	19.5	19.8	19.6	19.4	15.8	11.2	9.5
Trashigang east	max	20.4	21.7	24.8	28.3	30.0	30.7	31.5	30.2	30.0	29.1	26.1	23.0
	min	10.5	11.5	14.4	17.0	22.6	22.6	23.1	22.7	21.9	17.7	13.6	11.6

Southern Zone

The southern zone has a hot and humid subtropical climate with a monsoon season that is consistent throughout the year. The southern region also receives a significant amount of rain, and heavy rainfall can sometimes cause landslides and render roads impassable.

Humid weather in southern Bhutan

Places of Interest

Driving time between various places in Bhutan

From	To	Distance (km)	Time (Approx.)
Thimphu	Paro	54	1 hr
Thimphu	Phuentsholing	176	6 hrs
Thimphu	Wangdue Phodrang	70	2 hrs
Thimphu	Haa	114	4 hrs
Thimphu	Phobjikha Valley (Gangtey)	135	4 hrs 30 mins
Thimphu	Bumthang	270	8 hrs 30 mins
Thimphu	Punakha	84	3 hrs
Thimphu	Gelephu	242	6 hrs 30 mins
Punakha	Wangdue Phodrang	23	45 min
Wangdue Phodrang	Trongsa	129	4 hrs 30 mins
Trongsa	Bumthang	68	2 hrs 30 mins
Bumthang	Mongar	193	7 hrs
Mongar	Lhuentse	75	2 hrs 30 mins
Mongar	Trashigang	91	3 hrs 30 mins
Trashigang	Trashiyangtse	55	1 hr 30 mins
Trashigang	Samdrup Jongkhar	180	6 hrs 30 mins

Thimphu

Thimphu is the capital of Bhutan and the largest city in the country, located in the western region. It is also the political and economic hub of the country that houses most of the important government buildings and constitutional agencies. Many of the locals from rural places migrate to Thimphu to seek employment. This vibrant city contains a rustic charm that has much to offer to travellers. It is the seat of government of Bhutan, with an ancient dzong and a more recent House of Parliament nearby. You can also find many cafes and handicraft shops around Thimphu town.

Attractions

- Buddha Dordenma
- Tashichho Dzong
- Jungshi Handmade Paper Factory
- Royal Textile Academy
- Simply Bhutan
- Folk Heritage Museum
- Motithang Takin Preserve
- Bhutan Postal Museum
- National Memorial Chorten
- Simtokha Dzong
- Dochula Pass
- Druk Wangyal Lhakhang

Buddha Dordenma — a place for spiritual seekers and contemplation

Buddha Dordenma

Buddha Dordenma, also known as Buddha Point, is a famous attraction in Bhutan. This sitting Buddha statue that measures 51.5 m in height is one of the largest sitting Buddha statues in the world.

The Buddha Dordenma statue is made of solid bronze and gilded with paint, as are all of the 125,000 smaller Buddha statues placed within the giant statue; 100,000 of the statues are 8 inches tall, and 25,000 of the statues are 12 inches tall.

You can visit the majestic meditation hall with beautifully carved pillars painted in gold. There is also a gold statue of the four-faced Buddha inside the hall. Walls are elegantly painted with murals of various stories of the life of the Buddha.

From Buddha Point, you get an overview of the beautiful Thimphu city.

Tashichho Dzong

Tashichho Dzong, or commonly known as Thimphu Dzong, is an impressive structure situated in the northern part of Thimphu city that plays the dual role of housing the administration of the state and the clergy. Tashichho Dzong has been the seat of the government since 1952. It currently houses the throne room and offices of the King of Bhutan, the cabinet secretariat, and the ministries of home affairs and finance.

As a tourist, you will not be allowed to visit the offices in the dzong. But you can visit the monastery in the dzong, which is home to the Chief Abbot of Bhutan and a retinue of monks during most of the year. The clergy moves to the Punakha Dzong in the winter, where the climate is warmer.

If you visit Bhutan between April to July, you may see a stretch of colourful rhododendron flowers greeting you along the pathway of the dzong. Alternatively, if you visit in March, you may also be in luck and see the blooming cherry trees!

You can explore the surroundings of the dzong and admire the marvellous architecture. Interestingly, you can also find a replica of the original Tashichho Dzong in Kagawa, Shikoku in Japan.

The much celebrated Thimphu Tshechu held at Tashichho Dzong attracts large crowds every autumn

Jungshi Handmade Paper Factory

Pay a visit to Jungshi Handmade Paper Factory to watch the making of authentic Bhutanese paper known as dey-sho. For many generations, Bhutanese practised the traditional method of producing dey-sho papers from the bark of the Daphne tree.

This ancient craft is one of the thirteen traditional arts of Bhutan that the country preserves. Bhutanese originally used dey-sho papers in monasteries for woodblock printing, manuscripts, and prayer books.

In the factory, you can also find other paper products like stationeries, greeting cards and journals that make unique souvenirs.

You can try your hand at this ancient craft and make some traditional papers of your own

Royal Textile Academy

Weaving stands as an indispensable cornerstone of Bhutanese culture and tradition, a craft that embodies the nation's heritage and artistic legacy. Amidst this rich tapestry of Bhutan's textile history, the Royal Textile Academy (RTA) emerges as a pioneering institution, singularly devoted to the preservation, promotion, and education surrounding Bhutanese textiles.

RTA is Bhutan's sole textile museum, a treasure trove of exhibitions that continuously unveil the fascinating world of Bhutanese weaving. A visit to RTA is an opportunity to immerse yourself in the intricate and captivating realm of Bhutanese textiles, where every thread carries stories of tradition, craftsmanship, and symbolism.

At RTA, the narrative of Bhutanese textile heritage unfolds before you. You can delve into the diverse weaving styles that flourish in every corner of the country, each district boasting its distinct patterns and techniques. A trip to the textile museum offers a profound insight into the artistic mastery that goes into creating the beautiful traditional attire worn by the locals, the kira for women and the gho for men.

Beyond its role as a museum, RTA takes on a dynamic role in nurturing the future of Bhutanese textile craftsmanship. The institution houses a Weaving School, where aspiring students embark on a journey to master the ancient art of weaving. Here, they learn not only the traditional techniques but also delve into the nuances of yarn dyeing and contemporary design.

Tango Monastery

Tango Monastery, located on the outskirts of Thimphu, was established in the 13th century. In the local language, "Tango" translates to "horse."

The monastery is constructed in the traditional dzong style, featuring a distinctive curved outer wall and a prominent central tower with recesses. It encompasses the caves where saints have practiced meditation and performed miracles since the 12th century. Etched slates can be found behind a row of prayer wheels.

The hike to Tango Monastery, an offbeat yet delightful excursion, typically takes around two hours, depending on your fitness level.

The path is well-maintained and not excessively steep. Along the way, you'll encounter a picturesque trail lined with pine and rhododendron trees, vibrant prayer flags, rest areas, prayer wheels, chortens, and meditation huts.

If you are exploring Thimphu on your own, you may consider getting a taxi to drop you off at Dodeyna, the base of the hike. However, finding a taxi to take you back may be challenging though. It's best for you to book your trip through a tour operator and include it in your itinerary. Additionally, you'll also be accompanied by a local guide.

Folk Heritage Museum

The Folk Heritage Museum is set inside a three-storey 19th-century traditional house. The museum provides visitors with a glimpse of the traditional Bhutanese lifestyle and artefacts in a conventional household.

The museum perfectly recaptures the rural setting and ambience of a traditional household. There's a collection of household objects, tools and equipment found in a typical Bhutanese home with paddy, wheat and millet fields set up outdoors and a traditional water-mill with millstones that are more than 150 years old. There is a traditional kitchen and a hot stone bath that is famous on farmsteads throughout the country.

Visiting the museum will allow you to learn more about Bhutanese culture, customs and traditions.

Artisan Pema Tshering refined the art of woodcarving after studying at the Institute of Zorig Chusum, where Queen Mother Ashi Tshering Pem supported his education

Simply Bhutan

Simply Bhutan is an interactive museum that offers you an excellent guided introduction to different aspects of traditional Bhutanese life.

This is an excellent place for your induction into Bhutan. You will learn how to dress up in Bhutanese traditional dress, distil ara (rice wine), and understand how Bhutanese construct their homes out of rammed earth. At the museum, you can also enjoy some local butter tea while watching local dance performances.

The museum primarily is a unique example of ancient Bhutanese architecture. The museum's structure was built reusing old timber, door and window frames, and numerous other materials from demolished houses.

Unlike most museums where you cannot touch the artefacts or take photographs, you can snap away freely here. You can also try a hand at archery and the local dart game known as *khuru*.

At the museum, you'll get to meet Pema Tshering, a talented foot artist who has been diagnosed with cerebral palsy. There is a little shop inside Simply Bhutan where Pema does his wood carving and painting using his foot. If you see him, don't hesitate to say hello or support his artwork.

Do check out the inspiring story of Pema Tshering.

s.bn.sg/pematshering

Motithang Takin Preserve

Motithang Takin Preserve is a wildlife reserve for takins, the national animal of Bhutan.

Legend has it that the famous spiritual master, Drukpa Kuenley, also known as the 'Divine Madman', is responsible for creating this unique creature, a gnu goat that resembles an ox but is more closely related to a sheep.

One day during the 15th century, people in Bhutan asked Drukpa Kuenley to perform a miracle at the end of a feast. So, he took the head of a goat, fixed it to a cow's skeletons, and with a snap, created the takin.

Some claim that the takin is the most queer-looking animal that they have ever seen!

There is a newly constructed skywalk at the Takin Preserve where you can spot the takins from above.

After visiting the Takin Preserve, ask your guide to bring you to the Bhutan Broadcasting Station (BBS) Tower. A five to ten minutes drive to the upper part of the road will lead to Sangaygang BBS Tower at 2,685 m. Colourful prayer flags are strung around the trees above the BBS Tower. From here, you'll get a picturesque photo background of the entire Thimphu city.

Druk Wangditse Lhakang

After your visit to Sangaygang, you may also consider hiking to Druk Wangditse Lhakhang. The hiking trail is considered one of the easiest hiking trails in Bhutan. It is located only 40-minute walk away from Sangaygang BBS Tower.

Druk Wangditse is one of the oldest temples in Thimphu. In the aftermath of the 2011 Himalayan earthquake, the initial temple endured significant destruction. However, it has subsequently undergone reconstruction,

Discover one of nature's wonders — Bhutan's national animal, the Takin

drawing inspiration from a depiction of the earlier temple made by Samuel Davis, who explored Bhutan in 1783, along with the assistance of archaeological discoveries.

The temple was restored to its former glory in January 2020 after five and half years of renovation. The interior design is impressive and the temple houses the original large gilt copper image of Shakyamuni Buddha.

The vicinity provides excellent views of the Samteling Palace, home of the fourth King, Tashichho Dzong and panoramic view of Thimphu Valley.

Centenary Farmer's Market

The Centenary Farmers' Market (CFM) has newly been renovated and transformed into a bustling center, catering to both farmers and consumers. Its contemporary design seamlessly integrates with traditional elements, showcasing Bhutan's unique cultural heritage. In the market, you can find a diverse array of fresh, locally-sourced produce such as fruits, vegetables, grains, and dairy products.

Bhutan Postal Museum

The Bhutan Postal Museum is home to the world's largest photo book and most bizarre collection of Bhutanese stamps that will intrigue any philatelist. There are five galleries in the museum that trace the development of the Bhutanese postal system, from the earliest mail runners who delivered mail to the remotest villages to Bhutan's most unusual stamps. There are also historical reminders of the time when people still hand-wrote letters and stuck stamps on them to share news.

One of the most interesting things you can do in Bhutan is to get your own personalised legitimate stamps at the General Post Office for Nu. 500 (around USD7). It contains 12 stamps with a mix value of Nu. 30, Nu. 45 and Nu. 50.

Go ahead to pick up some postcards, send greetings, and share some Bhutanese love with your family and friends.

Create your personalised stamps in Bhutan

National Memorial Chorten

The National Memorial Chorten is a prominent stupa erected in 1974 in honour of the Father of Modern Bhutan, the third King, Jigme Dorji Wangchuck. The stupa is a famous landmark located in the heart of Thimphu city with its golden spire and bells.

The Memorial Chorten is designed in a classical style of stupas with a pyramidal pillar crowned by a crescent moon and sun. A distinctive feature of the chorten is the outward flaring of the rounded part, giving it a pyramidal shape instead of a dome shape.

The memorial chorten is a popular site for meditation

Simtokha Dzong

Simtokha Dzong is the first fortress to be built in the kingdom in the 17th century and the first building to incorporate monastic and administrative centres in Bhutan. The central tower is three-storey high, with prayer wheels surrounding the courtyard. An interesting feature of the *dzong* is that the courtyard has more than 300 slate carvings that depict Buddhist figures.

On top of being an important historical monument, it also houses one of Bhutan's top-ranking Dzongkha language institutes.

Visiting Simtokha Dzong will give you insights into Bhutan's early days when Zhabdrung Ngawang Namgyal first unified Bhutan nearly four centuries ago.

Do remember to circumambulate in a clockwise direction, as with any religious structure in Bhutan.

Simtokha Dzong has been restored to its former state through careful conservation

On a clear day, you can see a stunning panorama of the Himalayas from Dochula Pass

Dochula Pass

Dochula Pass is located between Thimphu and Punakha at an elevation of 3,100 m. There are two significant landmarks on this mountain pass; one is **Druk Wangyal Lhakhang** that was built to commemorate the centenary of monarchy in Bhutan.

The other is the **108 memorial stupas** built to honour the fourth King, Jigme Singye Wangchuck, for ensuring the sovereignty and security of the country when he led Bhutanese troops in 2003 to flush out Indian militants who camped on Bhutanese territory. Both monuments were built by the Queen Mother, Dorji Wangmo Wangchuck.

In commemoration of the occasion, the Dochula Druk Wangyal Festival is held annually on 13 December in an open area near the monastery.

The view from Dochula Pass is breathtaking. Weather permitting, you can even see the Himalayan mountains from the pass, including Gangkar Puensum, the highest unclimbed mountain in the world.

You can light butter lamps at Druk Wangyal Lhakhang

Punakha

Once upon a time, Punakha used to be the capital of Bhutan. It was the seat of government until 1955 when the administration moved to Thimphu.

Punakha is also the main district for rice production in Bhutan.

Lush beautiful paddy fields and rice terraces will greet you as you enter Punakha. The pleasing landscapes and significant sites in the district make Punakha one of the most popular tourist destinations in the country.

Attractions

- Chimi Lhakhang
- Sopsokha Village
- Po Chhu Suspension Bridge
- Punakha Dzong
- Sangchhen Dorji Lhuendrup Nunnery
- Whitewater Rafting
- Khamsum Yulley Namgyal Chorten

Khamsum Yulley Namgyal Chorten

Take a morning hike to Khamsum Yulley Namgyal Chorten, a picturesque chorten built by the third Queen Mother, Tshering Yangdon Wangchuck. You can reach this charming monastery with just a one hour hike through the woods and paddy fields. The chorten is an example of magnificent Bhutanese architecture. The Queen Mother built this four-storey pagoda-style stupa to protect Bhutan and bring peace to all sentient beings and the world. It offers a spectacular view of the whole Punakha valley.

Bhutanese craftsmen took nine years to build this elegant and sacred piece of architecture

Sopsokha Village

Before you reach Chimi Lhakhang temple, you will usually begin your walk from Sopsokha village, where some traditional Bhutanese farmhouses have now turned into art and craft shops.

You can find phallic symbol souvenirs in all colours, shapes and sizes in some of these handicraft stores! While these phallic symbols can be seen flanking doorways, hanging off rooftops or painted on the walls of homes, you'll never find the phallic symbol on the walls of any temples or dzongs. The bizarre sight of phalluses wrapped in ribbons may surprise the uninitiated but the unusual symbol has a spiritual origin. You'll learn more about the fascinating tales associated with the symbol when you visit the famous Chimi Lhakhang.

From Sopsokha village, you'll take a pleasant 20-minute leisure stroll, passing through a large mustard and paddy field to reach the entrance of Chimi Lhakhang.

You'll find your pace naturally slowing down as you walk through the beautiful rice and mustard fields.

Sunset at the picturesque rice and mustard fields

Chimi Lhakhang

Chimi Lhakhang, also known as Chime Lhakhang or the Fertility Temple, is one of the highlights of a trip to Bhutan.

This sacred temple is associated with the famous spiritual adept, Drukpa Kuenley, the 'Divine Madman', a term used with respect and even fondness. He is known for his bizarre and unorthodox teachings that challenged preconceived notions of society. A celebrated persona in the Himalayas, Drukpa Kuenley used outrageous means and behaviour to expose hypocrisies in society, often aiming at the establishment, including the monastic community.

Drukpa Kuenley is also associated with symbolic imagery such as the phallus and has come to be described as a 'mad' saint that has spread the striking and creative symbol of the phallus all over the country — from souvenirs, wood sculptures to murals.

Chimi Lhakhang, built as a memorial to Drukpa Kuenley, is a popular pilgrimage site. Couples from all over the world and many Bhutanese who have trouble conceiving children visit the temple to pray in the belief that Drukpa Kuenley will bless them with children.

Check out **www.chimilhakhang.com** for heartwarming stories of couples who have successfully conceived after they visited and prayed at Chimi Lhakhang.

Chimi Lhakhang is a sacred temple in Bhutan, famous for fertility blessings

Pho Chhu
Suspension Bridge

If you're not afraid of heights, definitely check out the Punakha suspension bridge, the longest suspension bridge in Bhutan. It's the perfect spot for you to capture all your beautiful social media photos. The bridge measuring 160 m long is located above the broad and rapid Pho Chhu River. Traditionally, the bridge was constructed for the monks of Punakha Dzong to visit nearby villages.

Punakha Dzong

This magnificent *dzong* is the second-oldest and second-largest *dzong* in the country. It was also formerly named Pungtang Dechen Photrang Dzong, 'The Palace of Great Happiness'. Punakha Dzong is one of the top attractions in Bhutan due to its beautiful architecture and significant history. The building was the seat for the Royal Government of Bhutan before the capital relocated to Tashichho Dzong in Thimphu in 1955.

If you seek an adrenaline rush, walk across the Pho Chhu Suspension Bridge

The *dzong* sits majestically at the confluence between the Pho Chhu (*pho* refers to female) and Mo Chhu (*mo* refers to male) river.

The coronation of the first King, Ugyen Wangchuck, was held in Punakha Dzong in 1907. It was also the venue of the famed royal wedding ceremony of the King of Bhutan, Jigme Khesar Namgyel Wangchuck, and Queen Jetsun Pema in 2011.

Do check out the vibrant Punakha Tshechu

s.bn.sg/punakhafest

You may see beautiful jacarandas bloom in the courtyard of the dzong between April to May

Whitewater Rafting

If you are an adrenaline junkie or a thrill-seeker, consider whitewater rafting in Punakha. It's a fun activity to do with friends and family. You'll be rafting through the crystal-clear river, admiring the incredible landscapes of Punakha valley. No prior experience is required for the rafting as long as you do not mind getting a little wet by the end of it. All, including children aged 7 or the elderly, can enjoy whitewater rafting.

* Advanced booking required and charges apply.

Whitewater rafting is a safe activity carried out with highly trained and experienced rafting guides. The activity takes approximately two hours to complete. The best time for rafting is in March, April, and between November to December.

The rugged, untamed waterways of Bhutan will not disappoint the adventure-seekers

Sangchhen Dorji Lhuendrup Nunnery

Sangchhen Dorji Lhuendrup Nunnery overlooks the stunning Punakha and Wangdue Phodrang valleys from the courtyard. The nunnery was built to serve as a college to train nuns and currently houses about 120 nuns. The double-storey complex founded by Yab Ugyen Dorji — father of the Queen Mothers — showcases the finest craftsmanship in Bhutanese architecture, skilfully crafted by local artisans. The nunnery complex functions as a meditation centre and offers life-skills training to nuns: *thangka* painting, embroidery, tailoring and sculpting. The temple is also home to the tallest Avalokiteshvara statue in Bhutan; the statue is 4.2 m tall. There is also a striking chorten resembling Nepal's Boudhanath Stupa in the compound. You can immerse yourself in meditation sessions and observe the nuns' spiritual practice in the nunnery.

Sangchhen Dorji Lhuendrup Nunnery has a nice, quiet and peaceful ambience

Paro

Paro is the gateway to the kingdom where the international airport is located. Bhutan's most iconic landmark, Taktsang Monastery and many sacred sites and historic buildings are also located within Paro.

Paro has the perfect blend of ancient beauty and modern charm. It is one of the most vibrant and dynamic districts in Bhutan. In Paro town, you can find stretches of western-style cafés alongside traditional handicraft shops.

Attractions

- Taktsang Monastery
- Kyichu Lhakhang
- Tachog Lhakhang
- Jangtsa Dumtseg Lhakhang
- Dra Karpo
- Kila Goenpa
- Zuri Dzong
- Paro Dzong
- Drukgyel Dzong
- Dobji Dzong
- Namgay Artisanal Brewery
- Aum Choden Homestay
- Chencho Weaving House
- Chele La Pass

Taktsang Monastery (Tiger's Nest Monastery)

Popularly known as Tiger's Nest Monastery, this iconic landmark of Bhutan is no stranger to the world. A trip to Bhutan is incomplete without a visit to this majestic temple perched atop the cliffside about 900 m above Paro valley. Seeing this spectacular monastery with your own eyes will make you wonder how they accomplished this architectural feat in the 16th century!

The trek up and down Taktsang Monastery can take anywhere between 3.5 hours to 9 hours, depending on your fitness level. Throughout the climb, you will see many locals of all ages, including toddlers as young as 2 years old, making their way up to the monastery. Parents carrying infants on their back or elderly with walking sticks are also a common sight. They will definitely serve as motivation for you to trek your way up to the peak!

It is advisable to start your trek early to avoid the afternoon heat. Remember to pack light and wear comfortable shoes for a smooth trekking experience. You can also rent a walking stick or hire a horse to take you up to the halfway point if needed. Above all, enjoy the stunning views and take plenty of photos.

A buddhist offering prayers facing Taktsang Monastery

Set on a rocky cliff high above Paro valley, Taktsang Monastery is one of the most impressive temples in the world

Tachog Lhakhang

Tachog Lhakhang, also known as Tashog or Tamchhog, is a small private temple located around 15 km into the journey from Paro to Thimphu. The temple was built in the 16th century by a renowned mahasiddha or practitioner of yoga and tantra, Thangtong Gyalpo. He is also known as the great 'Iron Bridge Builder' in the kingdom who built 58 iron suspension bridges, 111 stupas and many monasteries throughout the Himalayan region. To reach the temple, you will need to cross one of the eight suspension bridges he built in Bhutan. Crossing this ancient bridge is quite an adventure for some travellers.

Kyichu Lhakhang

The 7th century Kyichu Lhakhang, also known as Lho Kyerchu or Kyerchu, is the oldest and one of the most beautiful temples in Bhutan. Bhutanese revere the temple as a sacred jewel of Bhutan. The original temple was said to have been built overnight and used to be a smaller structure before the monastery was expanded. This spectacular temple has a tranquil and serene ambience that fosters a contemplative space. The elderly come to circumambulate the temple while chanting mantras and spinning prayer wheels. There is also a landscaped garden outside with an extraordinary orange tree in the courtyard that bears fruits all year round!

Cross the timeless old iron bridge of Bhutan

A majestic ancient temple from the 7th century

Jangtsa Dumtseg Lhakhang

Jangtsa Dumtseg Lhakhang is a unique temple located at Shari village in Paro valley. Unlike the other traditional Buddhist temples, the shape and design of this temple is modelled after a stupa. It is believed that Thangthong Gyalpo, the 'Iron Bridge Builder', constructed the temple around 1433. He subdued a powerful earth elemental spirit, and a subterranean serpentine spirit called a Lunyen. Both of them were malicious and caused much suffering and illness, such as leprosy, to the people residing in the area.

You have to be careful while visiting the temple as steep wooden ladders connect the floors and it is very dark inside.

The temple is a three-storey structure with each floor representing the three realms of heaven, earth, and hell, respectively.

A unique feature of the temple is the four sets of iron chains extending from the central tower and bound to the roof of the temple. According to local legends, the central tower, if left unchained, would fly off to Tibet.

You may need to rely on your mobile phone lights to navigate your way when you are inside

Dra Karpo

Dra Karpo, 'Split Rock', is a popular pilgrimage site in Paro valley. The location is believed to have been visited by Guru Rinpoche, who brought Buddhism to Bhutan, and his consort, Yeshey Tshogay. Since then, several Buddhist masters have visited Dra Karpo over the centuries.

Pilgrims circumambulate the mountainside 108 times over three to four days to gain merit and blessings. Of course, one can also do the short version of completing 13 rounds instead of 108; this will take about half an hour to 45 minutes.

The locals believe that circumambulating Dra Karpo will cleanse one's obscurations and bring about the highest level of spiritual attainment.

The site also attracted global attention when the international star Jet Li meditated there during his visit to Bhutan.

Kila Goenpa

Kila Goenpa is one of the oldest nunneries in Bhutan. In the 19th century, it was initially a meditation site. Fire destroyed the site, but it was restored much later by the 25th Chief Abbot of Bhutan, Sherub Gyeltshen.

The Royal Government of Bhutan established the nunnery in 1968. Kila Goenpa is home to nuns who are engaged in Buddhist studies. One can see maroon-clad nuns entering and exiting the buildings that were built precariously on the face of a cliff.

To reach the nunnery, you have to hike for an hour from Chele La Pass. The hike is mostly downhill, cutting through dense coniferous forests. The nunnery has seven small temples and several meditation huts.

Dra Karpo is a very holy pilgrimage site

The nuns at Kila Goemba lead simple lives

Zuri Dzong

Zuri Dzong is located above Paro Rinpung Dzong and the National Museum known as Taa Dzong. It is one of the oldest *dzongs* in Bhutan, built in 1352.

It was previously named 'Namthang Karpo' by Guru Rinpoche. Yung Toen Dorji, a disciple of Zuri Jampa Singye, later changed it to 'Zuri'.

In the early days, Zuri Dzong served as a watchtower along with Taa Dzong because of their strategic location and clear panoramic view of Paro valley.

Even though the *dzong* is smaller than most fortresses in Bhutan, the journey towards the *dzong* is highly rewarding. The hike is approximately 1.5 hours from the National Museum and an hour from COMO Uma Paro Resort.

You'll need to cross a small bridge to reach Zuri Dzong.

Zuri Dzong has one of the best viewpoints of Paro valley

Paro Dzong

Paro Dzong, also known as Rinpung Dzong, or the 'Fortress of the Heaps of Jewels', is a very distinguished building in the Paro district. You can catch a glimpse of it while your flight is landing at Paro International Airport. The dzong was built in 1644 under the instruction of Zhabdrung Ngawang Namgyal. Formerly, it served as a fort to defend Paro valley against invasions from Tibet. This ancient fortress is closely situated near Paro town and is easily accessible. During the popular Paro Tshechu, usually held in March, thousands of people flock to the courtyard of the dzong in their finest attire to join in the special occasion.

Some of the scenes from Bernardo Bertolucci's 1993 movie 'Little Buddha' were also filmed in Paro Dzong.

Paro Dzong is only a 15-minute walk from Paro Town

Drukgyel Dzong

The ancient ruins of Drukgyel Dzong is a famous archaeological site in Bhutan, located on a ridge in the upper Paro valley. It was constructed in 1649 and served as an important defence base in the region until 1951, when fire almost wrecked it completely.

Unlike the other ancient fortresses in the country, Drukgyel Dzong is the only dzong used for defensive purposes without any religious or administrative functions. The existing ruins and original defence structure of the dzong have been well-preserved through recent renovations.

The fort is located on top of a hill with steep cliffs on three sides and a single entrance to ensure that it is not vulnerable to attacks. It is heavily guarded by several watchtowers situated between the entrance and the foot of the hill.

There used to be tunnels providing protected passages for people to fetch water from the river at the foot of the hill, but these tunnels are now sealed.

Drugyel Dzong, a historic landmark that was crumbling with age, has now been restored

Dobji Dzong

Dobji Dzong is considered considered the first model *dzong* of Bhutan. Lama Ngawang Chogyal, the brother of the famous Drukpa Kuenley, built the *dzong* in 1531. The *dzong* is perched atop the large ridge overseeing the Thimphu-Phuentsholing Highway. Legend has it that Lama Ngawang Chogyal found a suitable site to build the *dzong* at the current place while looking for the spring source that originated below the throne of Jetsun Milarepa in Tibet.

Beneath the dzong, there is healing spring water trickling out of the rocky mountain. The locals believe that if one drinks or washes their heads and other body parts with deep devotion, the holy water will cure illnesses: headache, skin rashes, rheumatism, ulcer, gastritis, or stomach ache.

This 16th century *dzong* sits atop a ridge that now overlooks one of Bhutan's main highways

Namgay Artisanal Brewery

Namgay Artisanal Brewery is one of Bhutan's pioneer breweries in the craft beer industry. The brewery enjoys the distinction of being Bhutan's only brewpub and the second craft brewery operating in the country.

With a brewing capacity of 2000 litres, Namgay Artisanal Brewery has been churning out several craft beers that have become household favourites within a short span of time since its opening in 2016. Their flagship and best-selling beer is the Red Rice Lager, an easy-to-drink lager brewed with locally sourced red rice that adds subtle nutty notes and slight sweetness to the palate.

Inform your tour agency to book a brewery tour in advance should you wish to tour the brewery attached to the brewpub. The terrace offers one of the loveliest views over Paro Valley, and the golden hour light makes it a perfect spot for a photo.

They also brew dark ales, wheat beers, and apple ciders. These beers are available in any liquor outlet in Bhutan. However, if you wish to sample more beers that are not available in bottles, a visit to the brewpub is recommended. Apart from sampling the bottled and draft beers, Namgay Brewery offers other beers only available at the brewpub. Be sure to look out for their seasonal beers too.

Chill and unwind with some good local food and beers at Namgay Artisanal Brewery

Rimphu Heritage blends timeless tradition with homely comfort

Rimphu Heritage

Rimphu Heritage is a beautifully refurbished sixth-generation ancestral home in Paro where legends, heritage, and warm Bhutanese hospitality meet. It offers the perfect balance between peaceful countryside charm and easy access to Paro's landmarks.

The home once belonged to a respected trader, Tshongpa Gesha Tashi, and is now lovingly maintained by the sixth-generation matriarch, Angay Dawa Lham.

Each guest room will be offered a private bathroom and thoughtful touches that reflect Bhutan's hospitality. You can take part in traditional Bhutanese cooking sessions, before winding down to an enchanting evening of cultural performances under the starry Paro skies.

Meals are prepared in the family kitchen using fresh local ingredients, allowing you to savour authentic Bhutanese flavours. After a day of exploring, relax on the garden terrace overlooking Paro's serene valley.

Chencho Weaving House

At Chencho Weaving House, also known as Traditional Weaving House, you'll see skilful women weavers apply their impeccable skills as they weave textiles out of cotton, silk, and other yarns.

You'll also get first-hand experience with the looms used to weave the textiles and understand the processes involved in producing handwoven textiles. A wide range of handwoven textiles is also available for you to browse through.

Chele La Pass

Chele La Pass is the highest mountain pass in Bhutan at 3,810 m, situated between Paro and Haa valley. The drive to the pass takes approximately two hours from Paro. The journey offers superb views and brings you through thick, dense forests.

If you are lucky and the skies are clear, you'll see the magnificent Mount Jomolhari, Jichu Drake and other spectacular peaks from the pass. You'll be mesmerised by the stunning mountain views, fluttering prayer flags and lush green valleys from this vantage point.

You can find a vast collection of Bhutanese textiles at Chencho Weaving House

Chele La Pass offers a superb view of the Himalayan range

Haa

Haa is one of the most beautiful and pristine places in Bhutan, with untouched natural beauty. Another name of Haa is 'Hidden Land of Rice Valley'. It is one of the smallest districts and least populated valleys in Bhutan.

The Haa district borders Tibet, and is the ancestral home of the Royal Grandmother. If you are looking for a peaceful getaway, Haa district is a great option to unwind and embrace tranquillity.

Haa valley is also a paradise for hikers and trekkers as some of the best trekking and mountain biking routes are found around this area. The most popular festival for the Haa community is the Haa Spring Festival usually held in April.

Attractions

- Lhakhang Karpo
- Lhakhang Nagpo
- Shelkar Drak
- Chhundu Lhakhang
- Haa Dzong
- Juneydrak Hermitage

Lhakhang Karpo

Lhakhang Karpo and Lhakhang Nagpo are two of the 108 monasteries built by Tibetan King Songtsen Gampo in the 7th century. It is believed that the King had released two pigeons, a white and black one, to allocate the sites for the two temples. The area where the white pigeon landed was chosen for construction and named Lhakhang Karpo, 'white temple'. Lhakhang Karpo is situated at the foothills of three towering mountains known as Rigsum Gonpo, 'Lord of Three Families'.

Lhakhang Karpo houses the monastic body for the Haa region, and festivals are usually held in this temple. The architecture of the temple reflects its name as it is mainly white in colour with Bhutanese design. There is also a colossal door intricately carved to welcome visitors to the temple. Buddhist paintings and murals decorate the interior temple walls.

Lhakhang Nagpo

Lhakhang Nagpo, 'black temple', one of the oldest temples in Haa valley, is just a 15-minute walk behind Lhakhang Karpo. It is said that the black pigeon landed at the site when King Songtsen released it. Thus, the temple was named Lhakhang Nagpo. The temple was incredibly built on a lake, and one can access it through an opening on the temple's floor.

In contrast to Lhakhang Karpo, the temple is elegantly painted in black. And unlike Lhakhang Karpo, there aren't any monk quarters on this site. The only resident you'll find within the temple area is the caretaker who lives in a small hut.

Most festivals in Haa are held in Lhakhang Karpo

Legend says that a mermaid spirit resides on the lake

Shelkar Drak

A short hike up the valley behind Lhakhang Karpo is Shelkar Drak, 'Crystal Cliff'. Shelkar Drak is a small retreat centre perched on a limestone cliff. To get to Shelkar Drak, you have to drive from Dumcho bridge towards Takchu Goenpa. At the turn below Lungtsho village, walk for half an hour to reach the temple. Above Shelkar Drak, there is a flatland where it is said that the fortunate can see a lake and a variety of fruits.

Chhundu Lhakhang

Chhundu Lhakhang is one of the temples dedicated to honour the valley's protective deity, Ap Chhundu. A visit to the temple will help you understand the interesting history of the valley. Legend has it that Ap Chhundu was banished to Haa by Zhabdrung after an altercation with Gyenyen, Thimphu's protector. He is also said to have quarrelled with Paro's guardian, Jichu Drakye.

The views from Shelkar Drak are absolutely breathtaking

Legend has it that Haa Dzong was built to hold back the evil influences of the serpent deities

Juneydrak Hermitage

Juneydrak Hermitage, also known as Juneydrag, is a small temple dedicated to Guru Rinpoche. The temple is situated at 2,930 m above sea level. The hike to Juneydrak Hermitage takes about 45 minutes from Katsho Village. Locals believe that Guru Rinpoche visited this place and subdued a demon. It's also believed that Guru Rinpoche placed the eye and fang of the demon on the cliff. This cliffside retreat also houses the right footprint of Machig Labdrön, a female Tibetan tantric practitioner whose practice of Chöd has heavily influenced all schools of Tibetan Buddhism.

Haa Dzong

Haa Dzong was established in 1895 after the appointment of the first head of the sub-district. The dzong was meant to protect the adjoining border from Tibetan invasions. A new dzong was constructed after the fire destroyed the dzong in 1913. In 1963, the dzong was handed over to the Indian army to be used as an army training camp. And in 1968, a new dzong was again constructed and continues to function as the district administrative headquarters.

At Juneydrak Hermitage, you see different naturally formed sacred shapes on the rocks

Dagana

Dagana is a small district in the southwest of Bhutan, a place for nature lovers due to its picturesque environment. Over 80% of the district is under forest cover, giving it a rugged and impressive landscape. Located below the major valleys of Thimphu and Wangdue Phodrang, Dagana stretches down to Bhutan's southern border. It's also a paradise for bird watchers as it is home to various bird species. An iconic highlight of Dagana is the three sacred stone megaliths: Do Namkhai Kaw 'Sky Pillar Rock', Do Kelpai Genthey 'The Rock of Ancient Steps' and Tha Namkhai Dzong 'The Frontier Sky Fortress'.

Chhukha

Chhukha is located in the dense subtropical forests region of southwestern Bhutan. Phuentsholing, the main trade city in Chhukha and a border town to the Indian town of Jaigaon, is a dynamic place.

There are two major ethnic groups in Chhukha, the Ngalops and the Lhothampas, making the district culturally diverse. Aside from celebrating Buddhist festivals, there are also other festivals and practices embraced in Chhukha. An important feature of the district is the two hydropower projects: Chhukha and Tala Hydropower Projects. Tala, the biggest joint project between Bhutan and India, serves as the largest revenue of Bhutan.

Samtse

Samtse is a tranquil subtropical district that is away from all the hustle and bustle of the city. The district is located in the most southwestern region of Bhutan. The main source of income for these communities come from agriculture and the construction industry.

The district is home to a diverse range of flora and fauna. You can also find exotic animals like local elephants in Samtse. An important part of the district is the Samtse College of Education, established in 1968 and deemed one of Bhutan's leading educational institutions.

Shivalaya Mandir

The *mandir* (Hindu temple) in Samtse was rebuilt upon the command of the fifth King. To commemorate the royal wedding in 2011, the King gifted the temple to the people of Samtse. The temple was constructed with intricately carved sandstone and features marble statues of Lord Shiva and other Hindu deities. It was built around a sacred site where a small temple was previously located. The *mandir*'s construction was completed in 2015, coinciding with the 60th birthday of the fourth King, Jigme Singye Wangchuck, and consecrated on February 6, 2016, on the birth of His Royal Highness Crown Prince Jigme Namgyel Wangchuck. The 15 m high temple is an iconic site of the Samtse district.

Shivalaya Mandir is the first Hindu temple in Bhutan that is devoted to Lord Shiva

Tsirang

Tsirang district is located in the southwestern part of Bhutan along the Wangdue-Gelephu Highway. One of the country's longest rivers, Punatsang Chhu, also known as Sankosh River, flows through the Tsirang district. Nepali language and Dzongkha are spoken in the district as it is the central district where majority of the Lhotshampa population reside. In Tsirang, you can see colourful flowers brightening the traditional Lhotshampa houses.

Attractions

- Pemachoeling Heritage Forest
- Rigsum Pemai Dumra
- Hindu-Buddhist Temple
- Namgyel Chholing Rabdey Dratsang
- Birdwatching Point

Pemachoeling Heritage Forest

The Pemachoeling Heritage Forest was inaugurated in 2017 as an ecotourism site in Tsirang. The heritage forest is located around 30 km away from Damphu town. It is a sacred sanctuary rich with wildlife, such as the endangered royal Bengal tigers. The historical site serves to protect the natural forests and preserve the spiritual values attached to the site. There is a footpath from the ruins of an ancient fortress to a sacred pilgrimage site. The uphill hike takes about 30 minutes. The locals believe that a powerful king called Sang Sup Gyap ruled the ancient fortress around 200 years ago.

Hindu-Buddhist Temple

An interesting site in the Tsirang district is a Hindu-Buddhist temple situated right in the heart of Damphu town. It showcases the Hindu and Buddhist cultures that coexist harmoniously in the country.

The temple was built with two different entrances, with the Buddhist temple to the right and the Hindu temple on the left. Here, you will find one of the largest statues of Guru Rinpoche near the temple.

A Buddhist and Hindu temple uniquely housed next to each other under the same roof

Rigsum Pemai Dumra

Rigsum Pemai Dumra is a beautiful recreational park that is popular with tourists and locals alike. There are two huge gazebos, mesmerising fountains, a prayer wheel and an artificial lake for all the park-goers to enjoy. The park is a refreshing getaway from the hustle-bustle of city life. The park usually comes alive during the weekend with families and friends having picnics and get-togethers.

Namgyel Chholing Rabdey Dratsang

Tsirang Namgyel Chholing Rabdey Dratsang is the venue for Buddhist rituals and the annual Tsirang Tshechu. The annual festival is the biggest festival in the southern town of Tsirang. The masked dance festival, usually held in March, attracts people from all over the region.

Namgyel Chholing Rabdey Dratsang was designed in traditional Bhutanese architecture style

A beautiful blue-fronted redstart

Birdwatching Point

For those who enjoy birdwatching, Tsirang will be a paradise. The birdwatching point is located just above the national highway near Sankosh bridge. It's home to some rare birds like the rufous-necked hornbill, great hornbill, oriental turtle, grey treepie, paddy-field pipit, blue whistling thrush, jungle babbler, and black eagle. Even if you are not into birdwatching, do keep a lookout for these beautiful flying creatures. Aside from birds, you can also see a variety of butterfly species in the area.

Wangdue Phodrang

Wangdue Phodrang, also commonly known as Wangdue, is the last town on the west side of the highway before entering central Bhutan. It is the second-largest district in Bhutan and has extremely varied climatic conditions, ranging from the subtropical climate in the south to cool and snowy regions in the north.

Most of the district is environmentally protected. Wangdue Phodrang district is home to many rare and exotic animals like red pandas, royal Bengal tigers and snow leopards. There are also many rare birds such as the black-necked cranes, white-bellied herons and the spotted eagles. On top of that, the district is famous for its fine bamboo work and slate carvings.

Attractions

- Gangtey/Phobjikha Valley
- Gangtey Goemba
- Black-necked Crane Festival
- Thenkhor Yuetshe Trek
- Rada Lhakhang
- Gaselo and Nahee Village
- Rinchengang Village

Gangtey / Phobjikha Valley

Gangtey, also popularly known as Phobjikha Valley, is an impressive site in Wangdue Phodrang district. The picturesque valley is set against the backdrop of the Black Mountain range. It is a U-shaped valley with breathtaking views and abundant yaks that arrive from higher altitudes to seek warmth from the freezing weather. The lush green valley with its notable marshland is popular for its awe-inspiring sceneries. Phobjikha Valley is easily a tourist's favourite and a must-visit place in Bhutan.

Winter is the best time to be in Gangtey because of the crisp blue skies and chilly weather. If you visit during the winter season, you have an opportunity to watch the majestic black-necked cranes fly through the valleys. Do ensure that you bring along some thick winter clothes to keep warm. Aside from winter, Gangtey is also an ideal place to visit during spring due to the perfect weather conditions and beautiful blooms in the valley.

If you're a nature lover, Gangtey is a must-have on your itinerary

Tenkhor Yuetshe Trek (Gangtey Nature Trail)

Tenkhor Yuetshe trek is ideal for those who wish to take a leisure walk while traversing through a cluster of charming villages. It's a relatively easy 4 km hike that takes around 1.5 to four hours to complete. It's also one of the shortest nature trails in Bhutan. Your journey begins at the Gangtey Monastery and will take you downhill through the pine forest to a traditional village known as Semchubara.

You'll continue to hike upwards, following a dirt road that will lead you to Jangchub Kemba village. The path will continue through the primary marshland of the valley and ends in Khewa Lhakhang. You will pass through some spectacular portions of the valley.

Black-necked Crane Festival

The Black-necked Crane Festival is celebrated annually on 11 November, coinciding with the birthday of the fourth King, Jigme Singye Wangchuck. The festival showcases Bhutanese cultural heritage through masked folk dances and songs, raising awareness about conservation issues. It is a special occasion held at the courtyard of Gangtey Goemba where locals celebrate the arrival of the endangered and majestic birds from the Tibetan Plateau. T

he black-necked cranes are amongst the rarest cranes in the world and they migrate to Phobjikha Valley during the winter months between October and February. There is a Black-necked Crane Information Centre in Phobjikha Valley where you can learn more about the protection and conservation efforts of these graceful birds.

The locals rever the black-necked cranes as a symbol of longevity, peace, and prosperity

Gangtey Goemba

Gangtey Goemba or Gangtey Monastery is a beautiful temple located on the hilltop, overlooking the stunning Phobjikha Valley. The temple was founded in 1613 by Gyalse Pema Thinley, the grandson and the reincarnation of the great treasure revealer, Pema Lingpa. It is not just the locals who visit this humble and simple temple; the black-necked cranes circle the temple clockwise three times, when they arrive and before they depart from their winter home. How sacred and mystical!

The main hall in the monastery, known as the *tshokhang*, was built in Tibetan architectural style

Gaselo and Nahee Village

The two villages are located towards the western side of Wangdue Phodrang district. It takes about two hours to reach Gaselo and Nahee village. These traditional villages are ideal spots for you to picnic during the daytime and experience an authentic Bhutanese rural lifestyle. You'll get to enjoy the simplicity of farming life in Bhutan.

If you visit during early summer, you'll be captivated by the traditional methods used by the farmers during rice plantation. Autumn is also a good time to visit the villages to experience the harvest festival. You'll get to share in the happiness of the farmers over their bountiful harvest.

Rada Lhakhang

Rada Lhakhang, also known as the Temple of Sha Radap, is situated close to Wangdue Phodrang Dzong. It is dedicated to the worship of the local guardian deity known as Sha Radap. Locals often pay a visit to this temple to seek blessings and also for naming ceremonies. The names given to the newborns usually start with 'Rada'.

If you have a specific wish in mind, you can also visit the temple to roll some dice to see if your prayer will be answered. If the outcome of your dice is the auspicious number of 7, 11 or 13, it indicates that your wishes will be fulfilled.

Rada Lhakhang is a popular worship site for the local community

Rinchengang Village

Rinchengang is a small clustered village located opposite Wangdue Phodrang Dzong. The village is famous for its stonemasonry skills. It takes about 20 minutes to walk uphill to reach the village. From here, there is a great view of the dzong, valley and river. It is definitely worth a visit for those looking for a rustic village experience.

When there are too many carpenters, the door cannot be erected.

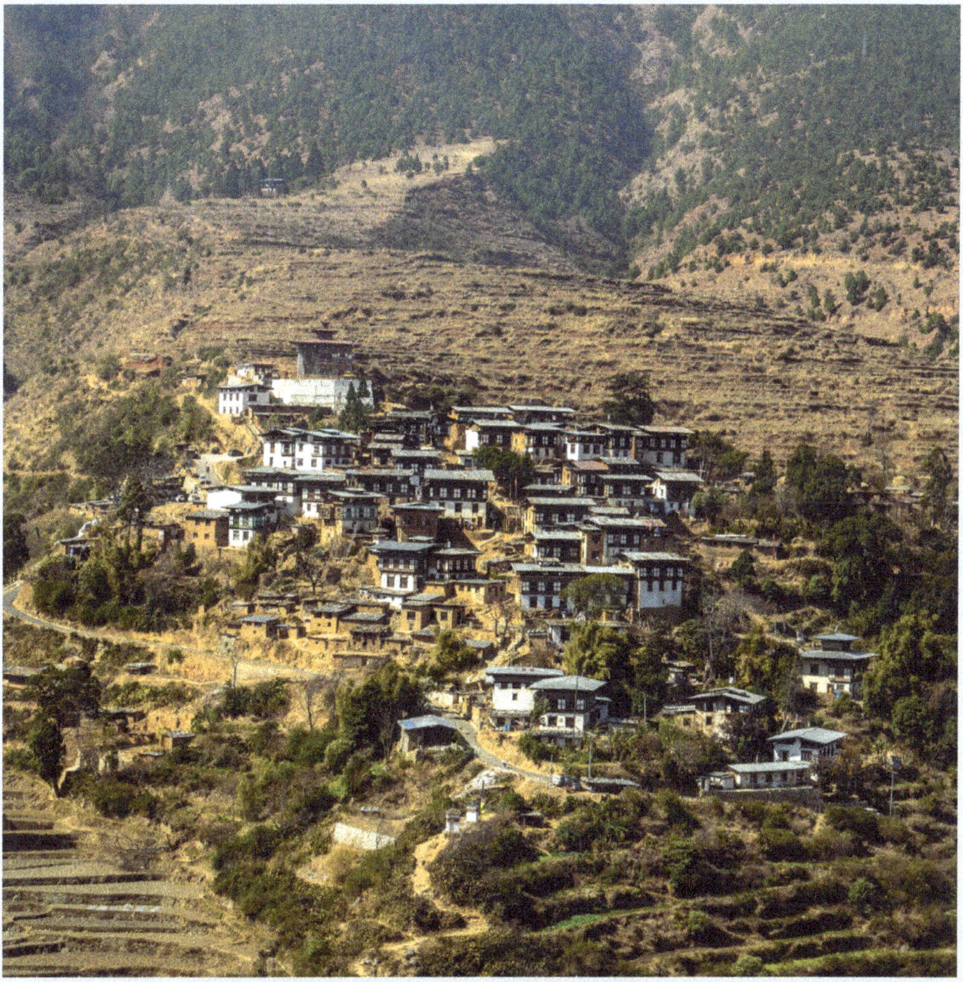

To get a glimpse of an authentic rural lifestyle, pay a visit to Rinchegang village

Gasa

Gasa is the northernmost district of Bhutan. This enchanting region has exceptionally long and cold winters and short pleasant summers. It has the smallest population in the country, with merely 3,000 inhabitants. The main source of revenue in Gasa is from trading products made from yaks. When you visit the district, you can find yak hair textiles, cheese, butter and yak meat. The community also harvest and sell cordyceps, a highly valued medicinal fungus.

In addition, the district is also well-known for its indigenous communities, the Layaps, from Laya village. Gasa is an incredible place to savour the natural beauty and tranquillity of the kingdom.

To experience Gasa, consider taking up some of the most scenic treks in Bhutan, such as Jomolhari Trek, Laya-Gasa Trek, Merak-Sakteng Trek or the world's toughest trek, Snowman Trek.

Attractions

- Gasa Dzong
- Gasa Tshachu
- Laya Village
- Lunana Village

Gasa Dzong

Gasa Dzong, locally known as Tashi Thongmon Dzong, was built by Zhabdrung in 1646 to commemorate the victories over the Tibetans. It later defended the country against several invasions in the 17th and 18th century. Unlike the other dzongs in the country, this ancient fortress is uniquely circular, with three watchtowers placed strategically to overlook the valley.

Gasa Tshachu

The hot spring located close to the banks of Mo Chhu River in Gasa is one of the most popular springs in Bhutan. Both locals and tourists often visit Gasa Tsachu to soak in the medicinal properties of the spring water. It is a frequently visited site in this least populated district of Bhutan, especially during the winter season. There are five bathhouses at Gasa Tshachu for the general public and one reserved for the royals.

On clear days, expect a spectacular view of the mountains from Gasa Dzong

Laya Village

Laya village is one of the smallest settlements in the kingdom, located at an elevation of 3,800 m. As of now, the only way to explore the village is via a two-day trek starting from Gasa town. The 28 km hike is not very difficult but you'll have to trek through muddy and slippery terrains to reach this mesmerising village. However, the good news is that a road is currently being constructed from Gasa to Laya. One day, you might no longer need to hike your way to Laya anymore.

Laya village has around 110 houses and is home to the Layap community. The Layaps have their distinct dialect and traditional dress that are different from mainstream Bhutanese society. The Layap women are easily identifiable with their yak wool garments and conical hats.

If you are a history buff, you'll definitely enjoy mingling with the semi-nomadic tribes to learn about their unique culture.

You'll also come across Bhutan's national animal, takin, or the exotic national flower, blue poppy in the village.

Lunana Village

Lunana is a hidden gem of Bhutan and the most remote settlement in the country. In the village, you can experience the culture of nomads living amongst the glaciers. The Lunaps make their living from yaks and sheep. The nomads are also very well-versed in medicinal herbs and earn extra income from cordyceps harvesting.

A charming feature of Lunana village is its unspoiled environment. During winters, Lunana experiences heavy snowfall and the mountain passes become inaccessible to the neighbouring districts. The snowfall causes the Lunap community to be isolated from the outside world for six months a year.

Healthcare and education is a challenge for the Lunaps due to the remoteness of the region. The government provides grants to encourage teachers to work in remote areas to help educate the children.

You can experience the beauty of this untouched gem by attempting one of the world's most demanding hikes, the Snowman Trek. Alternatively, you can also opt for a luxury Himalayan experience and take a helicopter ride to Lunana.

The two-day Royal Highland Festival, an annual celebration of nomadic highlander traditions in Laya, is a popular festival for the highlanders. On every 24 & 25 October, highlanders of all ethnicities congregate in Laya to showcase their cultures.

Check out Royal Highland Festival

s.bn.sg/highlandfest

Village life often revolves around yak herding, an important means of survival for the highlanders ·

Elevate your spirit and experience the Royal Highland Festival against the backdrop of awe-inspiring mountains

Bumthang

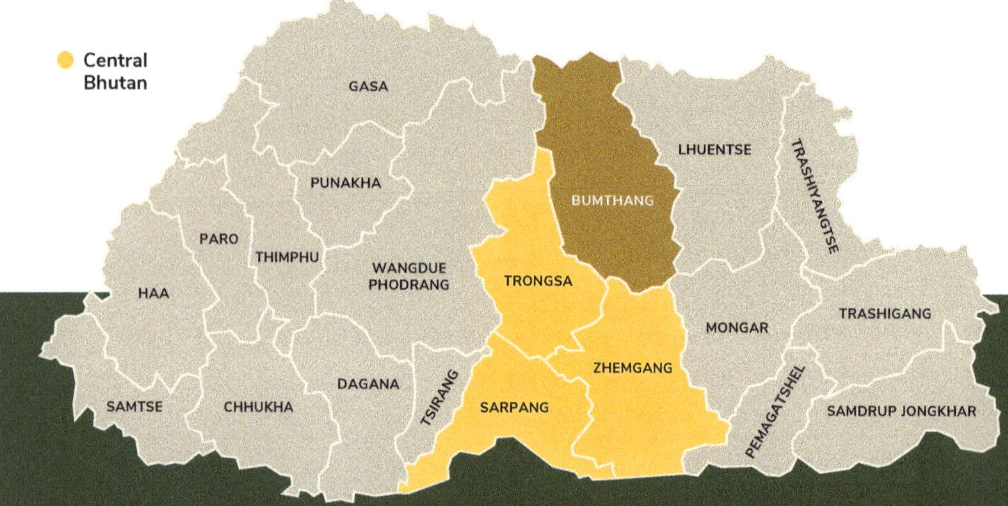

Bumthang, literally translated as 'beautiful field', is a historic district in Bhutan where some of the oldest and most revered Buddhist temples are found, including the 7th century Jambay Lhakhang. Bumthang, also known as Jakar, is located in central Bhutan. It was here that Buddhism was first introduced to Bhutan. The district comprises four valleys: Choekhor, Tang, Chumey and Ura. Bumthang is also famous for the production of wheat, buckwheat, dairy products and potatoes. Beautiful apple orchards and dairy farms are common sights in this district.

Bumthang is also home to Bathpalathang Airport, one of the three domestic airports in Bhutan.

Attractions

- Kurjey Lhakhang
- Jambay Lhakhang
- Jakar Dzong
- Mebar Tsho (Burning Lake)
- Bumthang Brewery and Cheese Factory
- Yathra Weaving Centre

Kurjey Lhakhang

Nestled on the side of a hill and surrounded by 108 chorten walls, the complex houses three revered temples. This large temple complex is filled with great religious significance. The main attraction of Kurjey Lhakhang is the upper floor of the oldest temple, built in the 17th century. You can find 1000 small statues of Guru Rinpoche at the temple. Locals believe that a path behind the wall on the upper floor leads to a meditative cave prohibited for public access. The cave is where Guru Rinpoche left his body imprint on the rock and meditated for three months in the 8th century. There is also a huge cypress tree near the temple entrance, which is believed to have sprouted from Guru Rinpoche's walking stick.

It is said that you can clear your bad karma by crawling through a narrow rock passage at Kurjey Lhakhang

Jambay Lhakhang

According to legend, this temple was one of the 108 temples built by the Tibetan King Songtsen Gampo in the 7th century within a single day. The tale states that the Tibetan King built a series of temples throughout the Himalayas to pin down the different parts of an ogress. Four were built to pin down her shoulders and hips, four more for the elbows and knees, and four to hold down her hands and feet. It was believed that Jambay Lhakhang was built to pin down the left knee of the ogress.

The single-storey complex is famous for its annual festival Jambay Lhakhang Drup as much as for its legends. The festival's main highlight is a sacred dance, known as Ter Cham, where masked dancers perform naked at midnight. In the evening, there is Mewang, a fire blessing ceremony where the devotees jump over flames to wash away their bad karma.

Jakar Dzong

Jakar Dzong or Jakar Yugyal Dzong is the dzong of the Bumthang district. It is located on a ridge above Jakar town in the Chamkhar (Choekhor) valley. Jakar means 'white bird', and Jakar Dzong is known as the 'Fortress of White Bird'. It is said that a white bird flew and perched on the ridge where Jakar Dzong is situated.

There are two unique features of the fortress that sets it apart from other fortresses in the country. Firstly, the utse (central tower) is 50 m high and secondly, the fortress has two parallel walls interconnected by fortified towers, which provide the population access to water in the case of a siege.

Traditionally, the dzong played an important role as the fortress of defence of the eastern districts. It was also the seat of the first King of Bhutan.

Jambay Lhakhang is an ancient Buddhist site

Jakar Dzong overlooks the beautiful Chokhor valley

Bumthang Brewery and Cheese Factory

The wide and open valley of Bumthang is the production centre for Bhutan's Swiss cheese and various local brews. A Swiss national, Fritz Maurer founded a micro-brewery and Swiss farm in Bumthang in 1996. Fritz married a Bhutanese and set up the first-of-its-kind brewery in Bhutan, producing draught beer, apple cider, wine, apple brandy and juice. This brewery also produces the famous Bhutanese 'Red Panda Beer', an unfiltered, preservative-free brew. The beers are prepared in an old-school manner.

There is also a Swiss farm that produces a variety of Swiss cheese and is the first commercial cheese factory in Bhutan. Check out the large round cheese on the drying shelves. They are often fully booked even before they're ready for eating.

Fritz Maurer is also credited for introducing modern farming equipment, green technology that is fuel-efficient, and smokeless wood stoves that are widely used in Bumthang and Bhutan today.

The brewery and cheese factory are located next to each other, so feel free to pop over for a taste of Bhutanese beer and cheese when you are in Bumthang.

Gigantic cheese made in Bhutan

Yathra Weaving Centre

Yathra is colourful wool, weaved with intricate patterns native to Chumey valley in Bumthang. Traditionally, every household in Chumey owns a backstrap loom and girls are taught how to weave from a very young age. Yaks and sheep wool is used for weaving because the thick fabric is ideal for the cold weather in Bumthang.

You can see women skilfully weaving intricate designs on their backstrap loom and dying wools using natural dyes. The women in Chumey weave throughout the year as it is their main source of income. Thus, yathra products such as jackets, throws and bags are souvenirs uniquely from Bumthang.

Mebar Tsho (Burning Lake)

This beautiful freshwater lake is a popular attraction in Bumthang. Colourful prayer flags surround the picturesque and legendary lake. It is said that the famous treasure revealer, Pema Lingpa jumped into the lake and re-emerged with treasures in his hand: a chest, a scroll of paper and a butter lamp that was still burning bright! Thus, the sacred site is known as Burning Lake.

You can also find stacks of tsa-tsas or small offerings around the lake area. Tsa-tsas are sacred objects moulded from clay mixed with the ashes of the deceased. You can find these miniature stupas in caves, underneath rocks, alongside the roads or any place sheltered from the elements.

Bereaved families commission these tsatsa offerings in honour of their loved ones

The calmness and serenity of Mebar Tsho will take all your worries away

Trongsa

Trongsa, formerly known as Tongsa, is the capital of Trongsa district, located in central Bhutan. Trongsa district was once an important district as it was the headquarters for the eastern region and the seat of the Trongsa governor.

Tradition also dictates that the king of Bhutan has to take on the role of Trongsa Penlop (governor) before becoming the crown prince and eventually the king.

Attractions

- Trongsa Dzong
- Chendebji Chorten
- Kuenga Rabten Palace
- Royal Heritage Museum (Tower of Trongsa)

Trongsa Dzong

The magnificent Trongsa Dzong is easily noticeable from anywhere in town. This ancient fortress was built in 1644 and used to be the seat of the Wangchuck dynasty before they became the rulers of Bhutan in 1907. This massive dzong is the largest fortress in Bhutan, located on a spur overlooking the gorge of the Mangdi Chuu river. The size, strategic location and grand architecture of the dzong renders it one of the most impressive dzongs in the country.

The first two Bhutanese Kings ruled the country from this ancient fortress

Kuenga Rabten Palace

An hour to the south of Trongsa lies the winter palace of the second King of Bhutan, Jigme Wangchuck, which is now the National Commission for Cultural Affairs. En route to the palace, it's a beautiful drive passing through Takse Goemba, several huge waterfalls, quaint villages and rice terraces at the lower Mangde Chhu valley. Stone walls surround the Kuenga Rabten Palace with courtyards on three sides. The tall main building is located on the fourth side with two protruding aisles.

The ground and first floors used to be a storehouse and a military garrison. However, the ground floor is now empty, and the first floor is used as classrooms for the monks. On the second floor, there are three adjacent rooms. The main entrance leads into the central room, known as the Sangye Lhakhang, the main temple.

Next to the central room was the private residence of King Jigme Wangchuck and Queen Phuntsho Choden. The King's room is still very well-preserved to this day. During King Jigme Wangchuck's time in the palace, other rooms on the floor were used as guestrooms and to grant audiences.

Chendebji Chorten

Like the stupa in Sangchhen Dorji Lhuendrup Nunnery, the stupa in Chendebji Chorten was also constructed in Nepali style. It mimics the style of the Boudhanath Stupa in Kathmandu. The stupa was built in the 18th century by Buddhist Lama Ngesup Tshering Wangchuck to ward off evils.

There are several legends associated with the chorten. The most popular one is that the Chendebji Chorten was constructed on top of an evil spirit manifested in the form of a gigantic snake.

A long prayer wall adorned with Buddhist scriptures is also located in the compound.

Chendebji Chorten attracts many pilgrims during Lhundrup Molam Chenmo, a festival held annually in the ninth month of the Bhutanese calendar.

Proverb

 མི་གཅིག་དགའ་བའི་བསོད་ནམས་རྟ་གིས་ཡང་འབག་མི་འཐེག།

Mi chi gawi soenam taa giya ba methey.

To give happiness to another person gives such great merit, it cannot even be carried by a horse.

Chendebji Chorten is also a popular picnic spot where you can simply sit down, eat and enjoy nature

Royal Heritage Museum

Officially called the Royal Heritage Museum, and locally known as Tower of Trongsa or Taa Dzong, this 17th century cylindrical five-storey tower is one of the top attractions in Trongsa. The first Trongsa Governor, Chogyal Minjur Tempa, built the museum in 1652. He strategically built the watchtower above Trongsa Dzong to guard the fortress from any attacks.

If you are a history buff who is keen to learn about the history of Buddhism in Bhutan or the history of the royal family, you should not miss this site. At the museum, you'll watch a 15-minute introduction video and get to explore 11 galleries. There are many interesting and sacred artefacts excellently exhibited on the five floors.

The Royal Heritage Museum is a fascinating site with stunning views from the top of the tower. However, visitors are not allowed to bring in their camera or cell phones.

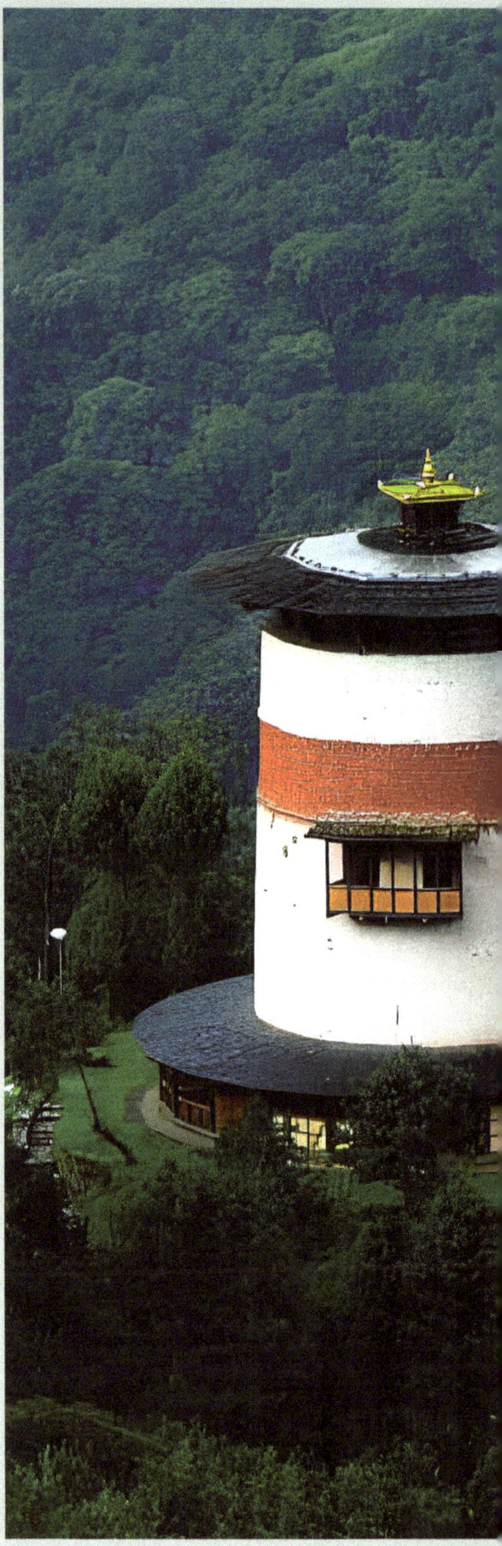

This is your opportunity to get up close to the Raven crown worn by the second King, Jigme Wangchuck

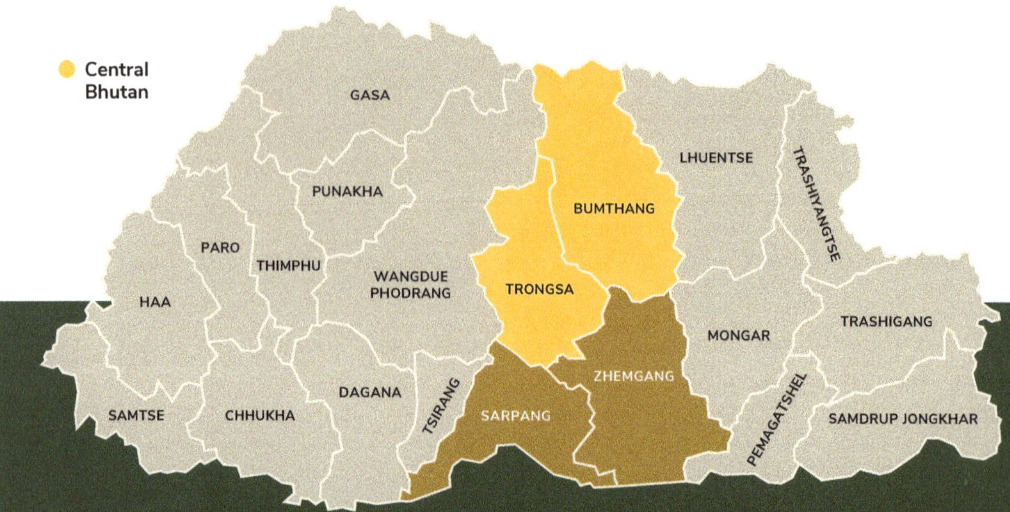

Sarpang

Sarpang district is located in the central part of southern Bhutan and borders the state of Assam in India. Gelephu is a major town within the district and is one of the three gateways to Bhutan from India. An international airport is currently being built in Gelephu town.

Sarpang is strategically located and has previously functioned as the headquarters for the administration of southern Bhutan. The district is culturally diverse, with Nepali being the dominant language spoken by the Lhotshampa community.

Zhemgang

Zhemgang is a district that is incredibly rich in biodiversity, with lush forests that are home to 22 endangered animal species. Royal Manas National Park also covers part of Zhemgang district. The district is known for being one of the last regions in Bhutan to follow ancient Bon (animism) traditions. Bonpo (Bon priests) are respected religious leaders in the region. The locals are also famous for their bamboo crafting and pottery skills. The local language of Zhemgang is known as Khengpa.

Bhutan Bird Festival

Bhutan Bird Festival is an annual signature event in the Zhemgang district. The district is home to 500 species of birds, including the White-bellied heron, various species of hornbills, and nuthatches. In addition to its diverse birdlife, Zhemgang is also inhabited by Golden Langurs and boasts the highest density of Royal Bengal tigers in Bhutan.

Many exciting activities are held during the Bhutan Bird Festival including, birdathon, art and literary competition, photo framing, trekking, fly fishing, white-water rafting, cultural extravanganza, traditional games, sight-seeing and camping.

Bhutan Bird Festival is an event not to be missed by birdwatches

Gelephu Mindfulness City

Bhutan is currently in the process of embarking on a major project in Gelephu, with the goal of transforming the city into a "Mindfulness City." This initiative involves establishing a Special Administrative Region (SAR) in Gelephu, which will play a central role in Bhutan's economic activities. The SAR will have the authority to create its own laws and policies, enjoying legal independence.

The primary objective of the Gelephu Mindfulness City project is to attract foreign investors and experts who are interested in establishing businesses in Bhutan. All businesses will operate by invitation only and must align with Bhutan's Gross National Happiness philosophy. This approach aims to create more job opportunities for local youths, offering international salary levels and enhanced access to technology and skills.

The Mindfulness City project will span an area of 1000 square kilometers, equivalent to 250,000 acres. Additionally, a new international airport is currently under construction in Gelephu to further facilitate the region's development.

During Bhutan's 116th National Day Address, King Jigme Khesar outlined the master plan and vision for Gelephu as a vital gateway connecting Bhutan to the global arena. This gateway will facilitate access to markets, capital, innovative ideas, knowledge, and technology that will shape Bhutan's future.

Samdrup Jongkhar

Samdrup Jongkhar town is located in the south-eastern part of Bhutan and borders the Indian state of Assam. It lies at an elevation of approximately 190 m and is known to be the oldest town in Bhutan and the largest urban centre in eastern Bhutan.

As a border town, merchants and tourists often use Samdrup Jongkhar to enter eastern Bhutan via land, especially if they intend to explore the districts in eastern Bhutan such as Trashigang, Trashiyangtse, Mongar and Lhuentse.

The road from Samdrup Jongkhar to Trashigang was completed in the 1960s, connecting the eastern and southern regions of the country. Given the road connection, the eastern region benefits from trade, primarily through trade across the Indian border.

Attractions

- Samdrup Jongkhar Dzong
- Rabdey Dratshang
- Zangdopelri Lhakhang
- Dewathang
- Mithun Breeding Farm

The easiest way to visit Samdrup Jongkhar would be to take a flight to Guwahati, India. You will need to apply for an Indian visa should you wish to travel to Samdrup Jongkhar by land. Your tour operator should be able to assist you with the arrangements. The drive from the airport to Samdrup Jongkhar will take approximately two to three hours. You will see the Assam tea plantations along the way.

Samdrup Jongkhar district in Bhutan is just steps away from Assam state in India

Samdrup Jongkhar Dzong

Samdrup Jongkhar Dzong is one of the newest dzongs in the country and serves as the office for district administrators. Unlike other dzongs in Bhutan, Samdrup Jongkhar Dzong was built on a flat and fairly wide-open area. The dzong was constructed in cement, a stark contrast to the older dzongs that were built in mud and clay bricks, with stones as the foundation.

Rabdey Dratshang

Next to Samdrup Jongkhar Dzong is the district monastic body, called Rabdey Dratshang, constructed in 2004. Rabdey Dratshang is the house for the monk body, and it has a number of new novices who are looked after by the religious representatives.

Mithun Breeding Farm

Mithun Breeding Farm is located at Orong, along the highway en route to Samdrup Jongkhar, above Dewathang town.

Mithuns are considered the finest breed of bison in Bhutan. These impressive cattle are well sought-after by cattle owners in Bhutan due to their easy maintenance and burly characteristics. Cattle breeders admire the mithuns for their ability to crossbreed with Siri breeds to produce superior-quality cattle breeds, jatsa and jatsum. These draught cattle are known for their high milk production.

Mithun Breeding Farm is the only farm in eastern Bhutan that breeds, raises and supplies mithuns to farmers in the six eastern districts of Bhutan. The farm is a popular tourist attraction as it provides excellent insights into the breeding process of mithuns.

Dewathang

Dewathang or Deothang is a gewog (village) settlement in Samdrup Jongkhar. Dewathang, 'Flat Area of Happiness', is a place with great historical significance, given its association with the Anglo-British war. Jigme Namgyal — father of Ugyen Wangchuck, the first King of Bhutan — led the battle against the British at this very site.

There is a bazaar in the village, and the army barracks of the Royal Bhutan Army controls the village entrance. Beyond the town, there is a technical college, a large hospital and a secondary school. Overlooking the village atop the hill is a Nyingma Buddhist tradition college, Chyoki Gyatso Institute of Buddhist Studies.

Zangdopelri Lhakhang

Zangdopelri is known as the 'Celestial Abode of Guru Rinpoche'. The three-storey temple set in the middle of the town is embellished with the work of master Bhutanese artisans. It serves as a spiritual refuge for locals to pray, make offerings and perform religious activities. You can often find elderly Bhutanese circumambulating the Zangdopelri. Its intricate frescos and beautiful statues are truly a sight to behold.

The architecture of Zangdopelri Lhakhang perfectly reflects its heavenly name

Trashigang

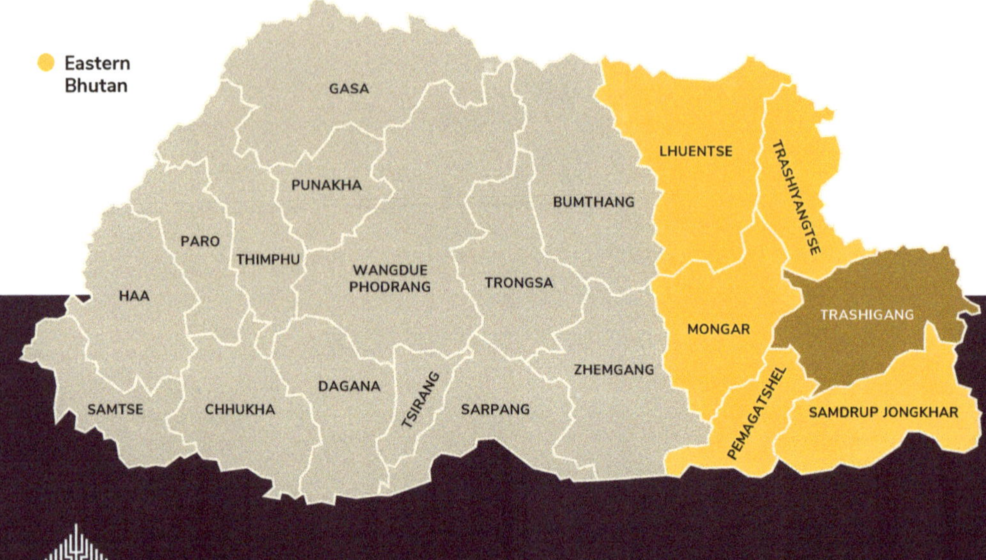

Trashigang is popularly known as 'The Jewel of the East'. It is the largest district with three sub-districts and fifteen villages, with altitudes ranging from 600 m to over 4000 m. The largest river in Bhutan, Drangme Chhu, flows through this district.

Trashigang is also at the junction of the East-West Highway with road connections to Samdrup Jongkhar and the Indian state of Assam. Furthermore, Trashigang is the principal marketplace for the semi-nomadic people of Merak and Sakteng villages. These indigenous tribes speak their own dialects and have distinctive cultures. They have a unique dressing style that is different from the traditional Bhutanese gho and kira.

There is also a domestic airport in Trashigang known as Yonphulla Airport.

Attractions

- Trashigang Dzong
- Khaling National Handloom Development Centre
- Radhi Village
- Khardung Anim Dratshang
- Rangjung Woesel Choeling Monastery
- Gom Kora
- Merak Village

Trashigang Dzong

The dzong was founded according to the prophecy of Zhabdrung Ngawang Namgyal. In order to spread the Drukpa rule over the eight regions of eastern Bhutan, he directed the Trongsa governor, Chogyal Minjur Tempa, to subdue the local chief and build a *dzong* at the present site.

Trashigang Dzong was strategically built and you can only access it from the north through a narrow path. From the basement, the dzong rises to a height of five storeys at the central tower. It houses several temples, amongst which Dupthob Lhakhang is considered the most precious and sacred. It contains the statue of Thangthong Gyalpo — the great iron bridge builder of the Himalayan region.

From the dzong, you can see the calmly flowing river against the mountains. The stunning views make this place a paradise for photographers.

One of the largest ancient fortresses in Bhutan, overlooking the beautiful lush green valleys

Radhi Village

Radhi village is renowned for its textile production, especially *bura* (raw silk). The village is also famous for its rice fields and weaving expertise. It is often known as the 'Rice Bowl of the East' because of its lush rice fields that supply most of the grains in the eastern parts of the country.

The village has a community of around 200 households where the people make a living from *bura* textiles during the off-agricultural seasons. All textiles produced in Radhi are made using the traditional backstrap loom and traditional dyes. Thus, Radhi village produces some of the highest quality raw silk textiles you can find anywhere in Bhutan.

Rangjung Woesel Choeling Monastery

Rangjung Woesel Choeling Monastery was founded by Dungsey Garab Dorje Rinpoche in 1989. The monastery exists to provide a conducive space for the study of Buddhist dharma teachings as expounded in the Dudjom New Treasure lineage, and to carry out dharma activities for the benefit of the Buddhist community in Bhutan and abroad. It has a flourishing community with four retreat centres and more than three hundred nuns and monks.

Khardung Anim Dratshang

Khardung Anim Dratshang, also known as Thakcho Lunzang Choden Nunnery, was built as a Ranjung Woesel Choeling Monastery branch.

This captivating and beautiful nunnery situated at Radhi village is a prominent tourist attraction due to its strategic location and scenic view. You can often see elderly women performing religious activities for the well-being of all sentient beings. If you are interested to learn more about Buddhism, you can also stay overnight in the guesthouse next to the monastery to observe the nuns' lifestyle and daily rituals.

Khaling National Handloom Development Centre

Khaling National Handloom Development Centre is situated between Samdrup Jongkhar and Trashigang and is easily accessible. A prominent feature of the centre is that it showcases traditional weaving and knitting of the unique Bhutanese textiles. It is also a great shopping destination if you're looking for Bhutanese handicraft or traditional clothes.

You can find more than 300 textile designs at Khaling National Handloom Centre

Gom Kora

The name Gom Kora or Gomphu Kora comes from a meditation cave where Guru Rinpoche used to meditate. Gomphu means 'meditation cave' and *kora* means 'circumambulation'. Gom Kora Temple is an ancient temple with strong cultural significance. Guru Rinpoche meditated here and left a body imprint on a rock, like the one in Kurjey Lhakhang in Bumthang.

The temple houses numerous sacred objects and relics such as a garuda egg, Guru Rinpoche's boot print, the footprint of his consort, Yeshe Tsogyal, hoofprint of Guru Rinpoche's horse and a phallus-shaped rock that belonged to Pema Lingpa.

Interestingly, you can also test your sin level at the passageway that leads from the cave to the side exit of the rock. You do this by climbing up the side of the rock, and they say that only the virtuous can make it.

Gom Kora Temple is a must-visit when you are in eastern Bhutan

Merak Village

Merak is a settlement in the far east of Bhutan, situated at an altitude of 3,500 m. The village inhabitants are semi-nomadic people known as Brokpas, 'highlanders'.

Merak and Sakteng were closed to foreigners until 2010 to protect the area's traditional culture from external influence. Previously, you could only access Merak through a two-day hike. With the road construction in 2012, visitors can now reach Merak village within three to four hours from Trashigang town even though the road is very rough.

The Brokpas were originally from the Tshona region in South Tibet, and they have resided in Bhutan for centuries. The Brokpa settlements are scattered around the village. The houses are usually a single storey built of stones with small windows.

The Brokpas have a very distinct culture with their own dialect and a unique outfit different from the traditional Bhutanese dress. The men wear a thick red wool coat called *tshokan chuba*. Meanwhile, women wear a red and white striped dress called *shingkha*, adorned with Tibetan amber, silver and gold. Both men and women also wear the *shamo*, black felted yak wool.

The highlanders sustain their livelihood by raising domestic animals such as yaks and sheep. Fermented yak cheese is a delicacy in the region. Brokpas either barter or sell their limited produce to procure other basic needs.

The Brokpa hat — that has what looks like five spider legs — helps to keep the rain away from their faces

Eastern Bhutan is a Shangri-la for landscape photographers

Trashiyangtse

Trashiyangtse is one of the newest districts in the country. It spans 1,437 sq. km of subtropical and alpine forests. It was formerly part of the Trashigang district, but it was separated in 1992. Trashiyangtse is the perfect destination for nature and wildlife lovers. It's home to some of the country's most important protected areas, such as Kulong Chhu Wildlife Sanctuary, a part of Bumdeling Wildlife Sanctuary.

The district is immensely rich in flora and fauna and a melting pot of cultures with diverse indigenous dwellers that speak different languages. The region is also famous for its marvellous woodworking and paper-making skills.

Attractions

- Bumdeling Wildlife Sanctuary
- Chorten Kora
- Trashiyangtse Institute of Zorig Chusum
- Omba Ney

Chorten Kora

Chorten Kora stupa was built by Lama Ngawang Loday in 1740 and has a similar design as Nepal's Boudhanath Stupa. Lama Ngawang Loday took twelve years to construct the chorten with the help of his devotees from the eastern region.

Legend has it that a princess from Tawang, believed to have been a *khando* (dakini) agreed to be buried alive inside the chorten to meditate on behalf of all beings.

There are two interesting festivals held here every year: Dakpa Kora and Drukpa Kora. During Dakpa Kora, the Dakpa tribe from Arunachal Pradesh, a north-eastern state of India, visit Chorten Kora to circumambulate the chorten. On Drukpa Kora, people from all over eastern Bhutan visit the chorten to generate merits and watch the unfurling of the *thongdrel*.

Bumdeling Wildlife Sanctuary

The sanctuary was established in 1998 and consists of diverse flora and fauna with magnificent scenery, including alpine lakes and the Bumdeling valley. There are more than 300 bird species, 700 plant species and 42 types of animals, including exotic animals like the white-tailed eagles, snow leopards, royal Bengal tigers, barking deers, Himalayan black bears and red pandas.

The sanctuary also houses important historical and cultural sites such as Dechen Phodrang Lhakhang and Singye Dzong.

There is a popular Bhutanese film, 'Chorten Kora' that recounts the legends of the site

Omba Ney

Omba Ney is also known as the 'Taktsang of East Bhutan'. It is built on a cliff and located within the holy pilgrimage site of Omba Ney, where you can see the letter 'Om' on the face of the rock. It is one of the three unique holy places linked to Guru Rinpoche, the others being Aja Ney and Hungrel Ney, where you can see the letters 'Ah' and 'Hum', respectively.

Omba Ney is a popular trek in eastern Bhutan, traversing broadleaved forests, chir pine savannahs, sub-alpine pastures, agricultural areas and small quaint villages. You can complete the hike in three to six days at a moderate to very relaxed pace.

Trashiyangtse Institute of Zorig Chusum

Trashiyangtse Institute of Zorig Chusum was established in 1997 in eastern Bhutan, under the then National Technical Training Authority. The institute aims to preserve Bhutan's thirteen traditional arts and crafts and promote the skills amongst the Bhutanese youths. Aside from imparting those precious traditional skills to the youths, the institute also hopes to create job opportunities for the next generation.

In the institute, you can watch students hone their crafts and support their efforts by purchasing their handicrafts that are for sale at the shop.

Trashiyangtse Institute of Zorig Chusum provides training in 10 of the 13 traditional Bhutanese crafts

Students can either opt for a 2-year certification course or 6-year diploma course

Mongar

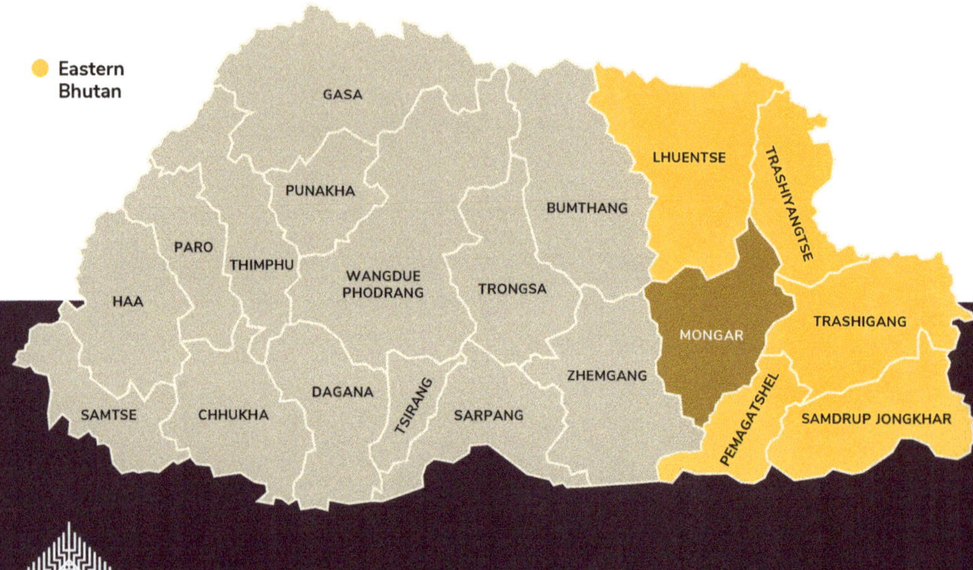

The road approaching Mongar is one of the most spectacular stretches in the country. It passes over sheer cliffs, then through beautiful fir forests and green pastures. Travellers taking this route will have opportunities to enjoy the bloom of rhododendrons. If you are lucky, you can even catch a glimpse of Gangkhar Puensum, the tallest mountain in the country.

Mongar is one of the fastest developing districts in eastern Bhutan. It covers an area of 1,954 sq. km with steep slopes and undulating surfaces.

The district is also famous for producing the well-loved lemongrass spray that you find everywhere in the country. The lemongrass aroma is a smell that many travellers will vividly remember even years after leaving Bhutan.

Attractions

- Korila Pass
- Drametse Lhakhang
- Mongar Dzong
- Kilikhar Shedra
- Aja Ney

Mongar Dzong

Mongar Dzong was built in the 1930s to replace Zhongar Dzong. The dzong is located just above Mongar Town on a gentle sloppy hill.

The dzong was built at the site where the master architect saw a white stone shaped like a bowl. Thus it was formerly called Zhongar, 'white bowl'. You'll be charmed by the beautiful view from the dzong.

Korila Pass

En route to Mongar from Trashigang, you will cross Korila Pass at 2,450 m elevation. You will see a charming chorten, a mani wall and fluttering prayer flags at the pass. Expect to travel through beautiful coniferous forests along the journey.

At Korila Pass, you can also visit a small shop nearby to offer butter lamps for your safe journey ahead. Lighting butter lamps is a common spiritual practice for Bhutanese. When a Bhutanese lights a butter lamp, they offer prayers for all sentient beings. The act of offering butter lamps symbolises the offering of wisdom and light to dispel darkness and ignorance.

Aja Ney

Aja Ney, situated in Ngatsang village in Mongar district, is another sacred site located at an altitude of more than 3,500 m in eastern Bhutan. The ney (sacred site) was discovered by Guru Rinpoche when he meditated in the cave for three months. A rock that bears the inscriptions of 100 syllables of 'Ah' is said to have been imprinted there after Guru Rinpoche completed his meditation.

Kilikhar Shedra

Located 2 km from Mongar Town along the Trashigang-Mongar road lies a beautiful Buddhist temple built on a hilltop overlooking Mongar Valley. The official name of the temple is Lungtok Choekye Gatshel Shedra which roughly translates into 'Hilltop Garden of Religion'.

The main temple of Kilikhar Shedra is a replica of Punakha Maachen Lhakhang in Punakha Dzong. Due to the long distance, people from eastern Bhutan may not be able to go to Punakha easily. Hence, Kilikhar Shedra was built in Mongar for pilgrims in eastern Bhutan to receive blessings with the same spiritual satisfaction as having visited Punakha Maachen Lhakhang itself.

Drametse Lhakhang

Along the highway between Trashigang and Mongar lies a notable religious site known as Drametse Lhakhang. It was built by Ani (nun) Cheten Zangmo, the granddaughter of the famous treasure revealer, Terton Pema Lingpa, in the 16th century. Drametse means 'the peak where there is no enemy' or 'peak without enemy'.

The temple is deeply associated with Terton Pema Lingpa and the Peling tradition of Buddhism. It houses a wide range of sacred objects and serves as a source of spiritual inspiration to the people of Drametse and the neighbouring communities.

The remarkable Drametse Ngacham, a sacred dance, has been performed for almost five centuries, and its influence has spread throughout the country. The famous dance depicts 100 peaceful and wrathful deities — performed in *tshechus* — originated from Drametse.

Drametse Ngacham is so special that it was proclaimed a Masterpiece of the Oral and Intangible Heritage of Humanity by UNESCO in November 2005.

Drametse Festival takes place twice a year at Drametse Lhakhang, on the 1st and 10th month of the Bhutanese calendar.

Drametse Lhakhang is a key spiritual centre in eastern Bhutan

Lhuentse

Lhuentse is one of the most isolated districts in Bhutan, located in the north-eastern part of the country. It is also the ancestral home of the monarchs and hosts a number of sacred sites in the country.

Lhuentse is famous for its distinctive textiles, which are considered to be amongst the best in the country. Women in this region are especially adept at weaving an extremely intricate patterned silk *kira* known as *kishuthara*.

Lhuentse also connects three major national parks in the country, Wangchuck Centennial Park in the north, Bumdeling Wildlife Sanctuary in the east and Thrumshingla National Park in the south.

Attractions

- Takila Guru Statue
- Pottery Farm at Gangzur Village
- Khoma Village
- Dungkar Nagtshang

Takila Guru Statue

One of the most popular attractions in Lhuentse is the 4.5 m statue of Guru Padmasambhava in Takila overlooking the entire valley of Tangmachu. The statue of Guru Padmasambhava in the form of Guru Nangsi Zilnon symbolises the subjugation of negative forces.

It is believed that the statue was built after the sacred prophecy of the great Terton Lerab Lingpa, who prophesied that, 'At one point of time, there will be a war of horses in Kurtoe Valley. To prevent the war, a statue of Guru Nangsi Zilnon shall be built'.

Pottery Farm at Gangzur Village

Gangzur village, about 2 km from Lhuentse town, is a small village consisting of 10 households. Lush green forest and spectacular mountains surround the village made up of traditional double storey houses. The pottery farm is well-known in the village, and you can observe skilled potters make earthen pots. This traditional craft serves as the main source of income for the people in Gangzur village.

Khoma Village

Khoma village is famous for their traditional weaving skills that has been passed on for generations. Their signature *kishuthara* textiles are highly sought-after all over the country. *Kishuthara* is generally used for *kiras*, but they can also be made into other products like bags, scarfs and table cloths. You can observe the exceptional weaving skills of the women as they create intricate designs and patterns.

Dungkar Nagtshang

The name 'Dungkar' originated from the physical shape of the land that resembles the shape of a conch shell. The house of Dungkar belongs to Trongsa Penlop, Jigme Namgyal, ancestor of the Wangchuck dynasty, the present royal family of Bhutan. The house sits against the backdrop of a towering mountain, overlooking the tiny Dungkhar village below.

There is also a temple, Dungkar Choeje Lhakhang, located in the village. The temple houses many sacred relics and treasures discovered by the famous treasure revealer, Terton Pema Lingpa, and great saint Desi Tenzin Rabgay.

The gigantic statue of Guru Padmasambhava in Lhuentse is surrounded by eight big and 108 small stupas

Pemagatshel

Pemagatshel translates to 'Lotus Garden of Happiness'. The district is notable for its artists, weavers and religious traditions such as folk dances and music. The tshechu festival in the district is also a popular attraction. Ausa, a famous folk song of the district, is sung on special occasions such as the departure of family members, relatives or friends.

The region is also known for its locally made sweet, known as tsatsi buram. The sweet is made from the abundant sugarcane that grows in Pemagatshel district and is well-liked throughout the country.

Itineraries recommendation

If you have only four days in Bhutan, you may explore the capital city, Thimphu and the picturesque Paro district. That way, you'll be able to check out some of the top attractions of Bhutan, such as **Buddha Dordenma**, **Tashichho Dzong**, and **National Memorial Chorten**.

Visit **Simply Bhutan** to learn more about Bhutanese culture and traditions. Print your personalised stamps at **Bhutan Postal Museum**. If you are an animal lover, you may also include a visit to the **Motithang Takin Preserve** to see the unique national animal of Bhutan.

Depending on how much time you have, you might be able to squeeze in a day trip to Punakha to see the magnificent **Punakha Dzong** and the famous **Chimi Lhakhang**. Stop over at **Dochula Pass** for the spectacular views of the Himalayas.

For the third day, hike up to the iconic **Taktsang Monastery.** A trip to Bhutan is said to be incomplete without a visit to Taktsang Monastery. Spend the remaining time exploring the charming town of Paro, where there are many handicraft shops and restaurants. You can also admire the night view of **Rinpung Dzong**.

Visit the majestic Rinpung Dzong in Paro

One week in Bhutan will allow you to explore Bhutan at a relaxed pace. You will have more time to admire the Bhutanese culture and visit more places. With seven days in Bhutan, you can spend two days in **Thimphu**, two days in **Punakha** and a day (or two) in **Paro**. You can also opt for an overnight trip to visit the small quaint **Haa** district.

To have a good understanding of Bhutanese culture and heritage, visit the **Royal Textile Academy, Simply Bhutan, Folk Heritage Museum** and **Jungshi Handmade Paper Factory**. Admire the grandeur of Bhutanese architecture at **Tashichho Dzong** and see the largest sitting Buddha statue in the kingdom at **Buddha Dordenma**.

In Punakha, you can visit all the major attractions, including **Punakha Dzong, Chimi Lhakhang** and **Khamsum Yulley Namgyal Chorten**. For a memorable experience, include some **whitewater rafting activity** (fees apply). Request for your tour operator to book the activity in advance if you are keen.

If you have ample time in Paro, visit **Kyichu Lhakhang**, one of the oldest monasteries in Bhutan. For an authentic Bhutanese experience, opt for a homestay or arrange for a hot stone bath (fees apply) experience. Of course, hiking up to **Taktsang Monastery** should be on your itinerary.

If you go to Haa, stop by **Chele La Pass** to admire the fluttering prayer flags and magnificent Himalayan range. Visit **Juneydrak Hermitage** and **Shelkar Drak**. Embrace the untouched beauty and serenity of the least populated valley in Bhutan.

Catch the glorious sunrise at Chele La Pass

A good ten days in Bhutan will bring you deeper into the country. If you have ten days in the kingdom, you can travel further to **Bumthang**, the spiritual heartland of Bhutan. In addition to the 7-day itinerary to **Thimphu, Paro** and **Punakha**, you will be able to experience the charm of **Phobjikha Valley**.

You'll have an opportunity to check out the beautiful **Gangtey Goemba**, and see the sacred **black-necked cranes** (November to February). Phobjikha Valley in **Wangdue Phodrang** is a perfect destination for nature lovers. If you enjoy walking, opt for the **Gangtey Nature Trail** and traverse through the Bhutanese villages.

En route to Bumthang, you may also stop by **Trongsa** to see the largest fortress in Bhutan, **Trongsa Dzong**. A visit to Trongsa will allow you to better understand the highly respected royal family of Bhutan.

You can spend two days in Bumthang to visit **Kurjey Lhakhang, Jambay Lhakhang** and **Jakar Dzong**. A must-visit in Bumthang is the popular **Mebar Tsho (Burning Lake)**. There, you can learn about the interesting history behind the lake and even meditate. Check out **Bumthang Brewery and Cheese Factory** to get a taste of the local cheese.

With more days in Bhutan, you can also do other short trails, such as the popular **Bumdra Trek**. Camping overnight in the wilderness will definitely make your trip to Bhutan an exciting and unforgettable one. Pamper yourself with a **hot stone bath** after the trek.

The lush green Bumthang valley in central Bhutan

With two weeks in Bhutan, consider a trekking tour such as **Jomolhari Loop** to explore the breathtaking Himalayan mountains. Otherwise, you can book an **east to west Bhutan tour**, exploring the less beaten paths. Your journey will begin from **Samdrup Jongkhar** in the eastern district, and you will alight at **Guwahati Airport** in India instead of Paro Airport. Do note that you will have to book your own visa for India (if required) should you opt for this arrangement. From Guwahati Airport, you will travel around 3 hours to reach Samdrup Jongkhar district in Bhutan.

Eastern Bhutan has a pristine environment that is unparalleled in the kingdom. It's a destination for those who want to experience the charm and simplicity of rural life — a magical place that exudes calmness, beauty and peace.

From Samdrup Jongkhar, you will visit **Trashigang**, the 'Jewel of the East', an incredibly picturesque district.

You'll be able to interact with the Brokpas to understand their unique culture, customs and traditions. Visit popular attractions in eastern Bhutan such as **Gom Kora, Khaling National Handloom** and **Trashigang Dzong**. You can also hunt for the elusive yetis in Trashigang!

Thereafter, you can visit the other eastern districts such as **Trashiyangtse, Mongar** and **Lhuentse**. At Trashiyangtse, check out **Chorten Kora** and **Trashiyangtse Institute of Zorig Chusum** to learn about the 13 traditional arts and crafts of Bhutan. Offer a butter lamp at **Korila Pass** and visit the **Drametse Lhakhang** in Mongar. Take a day trip to Lhuentse to visit **Khoma village** and **Takila Guru Statue**.

From Mongar, you'll travel back to **Bumthang** in central Bhutan and eventually make your way to **Punakha, Thimphu** and **Paro** in western Bhutan. Check out the 7-day itinerary for attractions in those districts.

Beautiful views from Khaling National Handloom Development Centre

Bhutan Essentials

Where to go shopping in Bhutan?

For the best Bhutanese products, visit The Craft Gallery, a store located in Thimphu town. The two-storey shop showcases some of the finest crafts by the local artisans. The Craft Gallery is a project of the Gyalyum Charitable Trust, initiated by Queen Mother Sangay Choden Wangchuck. Aside from promoting authentic quality Bhutanese products, the gallery also strives to provide a sustainable income stream for the artisans. Thus, by purchasing from the gallery, you directly contribute to the cause of various non-profit organisations and local artisans.

You can find all kinds of local products such as shawls, honey, embroidery goods, jewellery and textiles. It's definitely a great place for one-stop souvenir shopping if you're planning to grab some souvenirs for friends and family back home.

Thimphu and Paro are the best places to quench your shopping thirst. You will find exquisite *kiras* and *ghos*, colourful masks, prayer flags, handwoven textiles, Buddhist paintings, and traditional handicrafts in most of the shops. You can also buy popular products such as honey, cordyceps, wooden products or lemongrass spray.

The Craft Gallery

Norzin Lam 3, Thimphu, Bhutan
(Opposite Bhutan Development Bank Limited [BDBL]; behind Department of Revenue and Customs [DRC] and the Duty Free Shop)

Monday to Saturday
9am - 5pm (Mar to Oct)
9am - 4pm (Nov to Feb)

CSI Market

Gongphel Lam, Thimphu 00975
Monday to Saturday
9.30am - 7pm
Sunday
10am - 6pm

Nyemezampa, Paro 12001
Monday, Wednesday - Saturday
9.30am - 8pm
Sunday
9.30pm - 7pm
Tuesday - Closed

What can you buy from Bhutan?

Bhutanese textiles are a reminder of the rich Bhutanese culture

Cordyceps

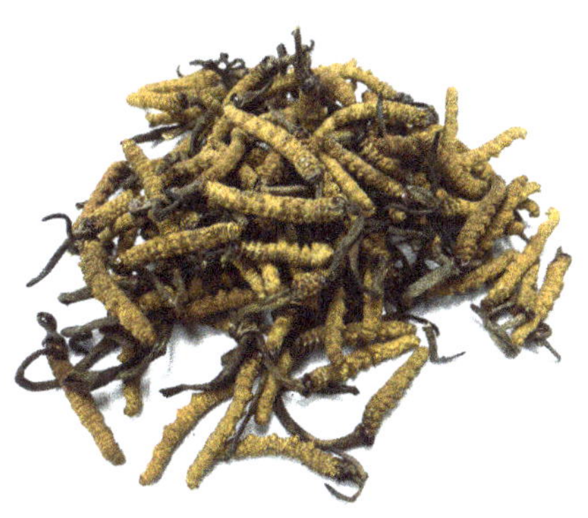

Cordyceps is a popular gift from Bhutan

Lemongrass Spray

The multipurpose spray has a long-lasting aroma

The K5 Blended Scotch Whiskey is the first and finest blend of whiskey in Bhutan. It is named 'K5' to commemorate the coronation of the fifth King of Bhutan, Jigme Khesar Namgyel Wangchuck, in 2008. The special recipe of the whiskey was discovered in an old distillery in the Himalayan mountains and assembled by distillers in Gelephu. K5 whiskey was produced under the Bhutanese Army Welfare Project.

If you're an alcohol lover, you can check out Drunken Yeti Bar. It's an amazing cocktail bar located opposite City Mall, Thimphu. Many claim that they serve the best cocktails in town. Alternatively, you can go to popular Mojo Park located right opposite Changlimithang Stadium in Thimphu to grab a drink and listen to live music.

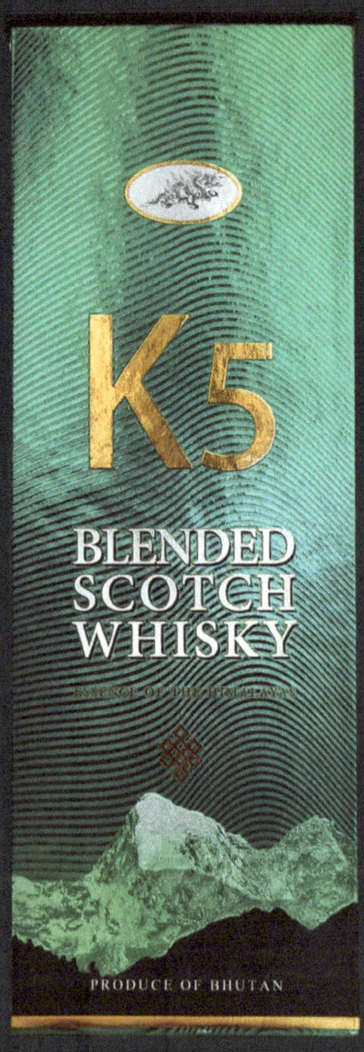

Bhutanese handicrafts are wonderful souvenirs for friends and family

Sacred wooden masks are great unique decors for your home

Frequently Asked Questions (FAQs)

01.

Is the Internet available and reliable?

Most of the hotels offer free wifi, but some may be limited to the lobby area. Internet connection is generally good in bigger districts like Thimphu, Paro, Trongsa and Bumthang. Some remote valleys may have intermittent connectivity. You should purchase a SIM card upon arrival in Bhutan if you want to have an Internet connection.

02.

Where can I purchase a mobile sim card?

There are two network providers in Bhutan. B-Mobile (Bhutan Telecom), which is government-owned, and a private company, Tashi Cell. You can purchase a tourist SIM card from the airport, mobile operator office, or any authorised dealer in larger towns like Paro and Thimphu. You will need your passport copy and 200 Ngultrum

(~3 USD). You might want to get an extra few hundred Ngultrum, especially if you want to call abroad or use the Internet. You can load your balance by buying recharge vouchers, which comes in Nu. 50 to Nu. 500 values. The vendor can assist you with the SIM card and data plan activation.

03.

Can I withdraw money from the ATM?

You may not always be able to withdraw any money from the local ATMs. It is advisable for you to bring along cash for out-of-pocket expenses.

04.

Can I make payments with credit cards?

Credit cards are not commonly accepted in Bhutan yet. You should bring along cash for payment. Most places accept payment in major foreign currencies.*

05.

Can I exchange currency in Bhutan?

Yes, aside from the airport, you can also exchange for Ngultrum at the Bank of Bhutan in Thimphu and Paro. However, they only accept 12 major currencies.* It's better to bring larger denominations for exchange.

06.

Do I need to tip in Bhutan?

Tipping is purely a personal affair. It is not the Bhutanese culture to tip. However, if you would like to tip your tour guide or driver as a gesture of gratitude, you may do so.

07.

What should I wear?

You should dress modestly, such as long sleeve shirts, full-length pants, and shoes, especially when visiting the *dzongs*, temples, or monasteries. If you are wearing a T-shirt, you will be required to wear a cardigan or jacket over it when visiting those places. You are also not allowed to wear a hat or cap inside the temples or monasteries.

As a general tip, it would be wise to always have a jacket with you when travelling in Bhutan, as you will be charting through different altitudes. Some valleys can be colder than others.

08.

Do I need to purchase travel insurance?

It is not mandatory to purchase travel insurance, but we highly encourage you to get one, especially during turbulent times. Travel insurance will protect you in the event of any unexpected or unforeseen circumstances.

*Bhutan only accepts 12 major foreign currencies for exchange: U.S. Dollar, Pound Sterling, Euro, Japanese Yen, Swiss Franc, Hong Kong Dollar, Canadian Dollar, Danish Krone, Norwegian Krone, Swedish Krona, Australian Dollar and Singapore Dollar.

Dos

- Dress conservatively (no jeans or revealing clothing) while visiting religious sites and government offices.

- Bring along some earplugs if you are a light sleeper, as there may be dogs barking sometimes.

- Remove your headgear and take off your footwear before entering the temples.

- Maintain silence in heritage or religious sites.

- Always walk in a clockwise direction when circumambulating a chorten, stupa, or prayer wheels.

- Always carry and produce valid travel documents when required.

- Purchase insurance in case of any unforeseen circumstances.

- Be responsible for your own waste and dispose of them appropriately.

- Follow traffic rules and use designated zebra crossings for your own safety.

- Always get advice from your tour guide if you are unsure of cultural appropriateness.

- Be respectful of the members of the royal family as the Bhutanese hold them in high esteem.

- Use both hands when receiving or giving any objects to be polite.

- Ask for permission if you'd like to take photographs of the locals.

- It's customary for Bhutanese to make a small donation at a monastery or temple. You can also offer a small donation should you wish to do so.

- If you purchase a *thangka* (Buddhist painting) or other religious artefacts, keep the receipts to present to customs officers upon departure.

Don'ts

- Refrain from touching any murals, paintings or objects in the temples.

- Refrain from pointing at sacred items, deities or paintings. Instead, use an open-palm gesture with your palm facing up.

- Do not sit with your feet pointed towards anyone older than you or at any Buddhist deities or statues.

- Carrying and using drones in Bhutan is strictly prohibited.

- Refrain from taking photographs or filming in restricted areas. Always check with your guide if you are unsure whether it's permissible.

- Refrain from feeding any animals that you encounter.

- Washing, swimming, or throwing objects into lakes or rivers are forbidden.

- Instead of handing out money or gifts, you are encouraged to form more authentic interactions and friendships with the locals.

- The exporting of antiques or any rare cultural artefacts out of Bhutan is prohibited. A permit from the Department of Antiquities is required.

- Bhutanese have a deep reverence for their religion, the royal family and the chief abbot. Refrain from passing any negative comments as it's considered very disrespectful.

Your Ultimate Bhutan Checklist

If you are travelling to Bhutan for the first time, it is natural to feel excited yet anxious, not knowing what to expect of this beautiful kingdom. This packing checklist will help you ease your anxiety and get ready for what might just be your most memorable trip ever!

Clothing

- Long trousers/pants
- T-shirts or long-sleeved shirts
- Cardigan or jacket
- Underwear
- Down jacket/windbreaker
- Sandals or flip flops
- Comfortable shoes
- Thick socks
- Hat
- Sunglasses
- Glasses

Electronics and accessories

- Lightweight backpack
- Camera
- International travel adaptor
- Water bottle
- Mobile phone
- Charger

Winter season extras

- Sweaters
- Warm jacket
- Winter coat
- Thermal innerwear
- Scarf
- Wool socks

Health and well-being

- Hand sanitiser
- Masks
- Motion sickness pills
- Sunscreen lotion
- Insect repellent
- Lip balm
- Toiletries
- Ear plugs
- Your personal medical kit

Important

- Passport
- Approved visa for Bhutan
- Copies of passport and visa
- Identity card
- Flight ticket
- Money for exchange

Check out FAQs page for the 12 major currencies accepted in Bhutan

Useful Websites

Bhutan Tour Operator and Drukair's Representative

Druk Asia
60 Albert St, #12-03/04
OG Albert Complex,
Singapore 189969
+65 6338 9909
hello@drukasia.com
www.drukasia.com

Treks in Bhutan

www.bhutantreks.com

Bhutanese Products

Chhom Bhutan
www.chhombhutan.com

The Craft Gallery
www.bhutancrafts.com

Cordycep Sinensis
www.cordycepssinensis.org

Independent News Oulet

Daily Bhutan
www.dailybhutan.com

Royal Bhutan Airlines (Drukair)

www.drukair.com

Department of Tourism

www.bhutan.travel

Emergency Numbers

Ambulance
112

Police
113

Fire brigade
110

Tips

You can remain connected to your loved ones while you are in Bhutan. Bhutan's country code is **975**. To call Bhutan from overseas, dial either 00975 or +975 (for mobile phones), followed by the phone number.

Transforming Bhutan's Museums into Living Cultural Hubs

The Museums of Bhutan, comprising the National Museum of Bhutan in Paro, the Royal Heritage Museum in Trongsa, and Ta Dzong, Trashigang are poised to transcend the traditional museum experience through a series of regenerative enhancements.

The Department of Culture and Dzongkha Development, Ministry of Home Affairs, Royal Government of Bhutan is fundraising to create outdoor museum spaces that seamlessly blend with Bhutan's Himalayan landscapes, fostering a deep sense of interconnectedness between cultural heritage and the natural environment.

Druk Asia is supporting the Ministry of Home Affairs in fundraising efforts to transform Bhutan's Museums into Living Cultural Hubs, with plans to build an outdoor amphitheatre at the National Museum of Bhutan, and an archaeological site in Trashigang. These outdoor museum venues are envisioned as sanctuaries for restorative healing, mindfulness, and community connection.

Building Fund

Museums of Bhutan

Visit **museums.gov.bt** to be part of something timeless — and to create a lasting legacy in the precious Land of the Thunder Dragon.

Illustration of the National Museum of Bhutan Outdoor Amphitheatre by Niimori Jamison Architects

Basic Conversational Phrases in Dzongkha

Hello

Kuzuzangpo la

How are you?

Chey ga dey bay yue?

What is your name?

Ming ga chi mo?

I am fine

Nga lesom bay ra yue

My name is …

Nga gi ming … in

What is this?

Ani ga chi mo?

Thank you

Kadinchey la

How much is it?

Teru ga tey chi mo?

I love you

Nga chey lu ga

What time is it?

Chutse ga dem chi ya si?

Where are you from?

Chhoey ga tey lay mo?

Nice to meet you

Nga chey da chebay sem ga yi

How old are you?

Kay lo gadem chi ya si? (formal)
Chey gi lo gadem chi mo? (informal)

See you again

Log jay gay

Basic Conversational Phrases in Dzongkha

Do you understand?

Haa goi ga?

I don't understand Dzongkha

Nga Dzongkha mishey

Can you speak English?

Chey English lap chu ga?

Good morning

Doba delek

Where is the toilet?

Chhabsa ga ti mo?

Good afternoon

Nima delek

I want to go to___________

Nga ___________ na jo ni

Good night

Zimcha delek

Let's go back to the hotel

Hotel na log jo gay

I'm sick

Nga nau mey

Can you help me?

Nga lu charo chi bay na mae?

Where is the hospital?

Menkhang ga tey in na?

Congratulations/Good luck

Tashi delek

Roger that

Las la or laso la

You will hear a lot of 'la' at the end of sentences when a Bhutanese speaks. The 'la' in Bhutan is not the same as the 'lah' commonly heard in the Singaporean or Malaysian slang. Using 'la' at the end of a sentence in Bhutan is a sign of respect.

It is delicious

Zhim tok tok du

Less spicy, please

Ema nu shu zhu gay la

More spicy, please

Ema mum zhu gay

Where is the money exchange?

Teru sosa gatey in na?

Is there wifi?

Wifi yue ga?

What's the wifi password?

Wifi password gachi mo?

See you tomorrow

Naba chey gae

May I take a photo?

Par chi taab ga?

Can I pay by credit card?

Credit card na pay bay tubga?

May I have the bill, please?

Bill zhu gay la?

How long will it take?

Dutse gadem chi go wong ga?

Is it far?

Tha ring sa in na?

Please wait a moment

Ah tsi tsi zhu na

No problem

Khe mi

Basic Conversational Phrases in Dzongkha

Yes, that's okay

Khe min du

Not okay/not good

Layzom min du

I don't want

Nga mi zhu

I don't like it

Nga mi ga way

It's nice

Ja chi chi

That's fun

Trowa du

That's very good

Layzom ee mae

I feel so happy

Nga sem ga yi

I love this place

Sa cha ga tok to du or sa cha di na ga way

I'm feeling tired

Nga wu duk chi

I love Bhutan

Nga Drukgyal kap gai

I miss Bhutan

Nga Bhutan drenmae

I am hungry

Toh kay chi

I am full

Pho dang si

Travellers' Tales

Travellers' Tales features exclusive Bhutan journeys by travellers from different walks of lives. Each of these travellers has embarked on a unique Bhutan journey of their own. Some of them have gone beyond their holiday and set roots in Bhutan, built a family with the Bhutanese or simply keep going back for more of the Bhutan charm!

Dino and Vanita

"We loved the purity of the country, its untouched beauty, and the locals' deep respect for nature and temples."

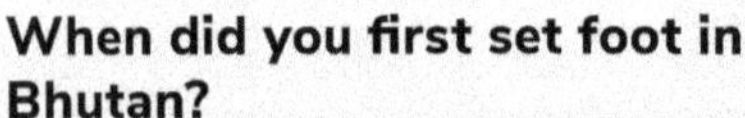

When did you first set foot in Bhutan?

The dream of visiting Bhutan came true in July 2023. We had the immense pleasure of visiting the country and immersing ourselves in the culture like we had never done before in any other place.

Why did you choose Bhutan as your travel destination?

We strongly believed that Bhutan would give us an experience made not just of beautiful places and temples but also a deep connection with the culture, the people, and the energies that reside in that beautiful land.

Where are some of the top photography spots in Bhutan?

Without a doubt, the temple Bayul Langdra and its surroundings, the astonishing Gangtey Monastery, villages around the Phobjikha Valley, and the Memorial Chorten in Thimphu share something in common. Even though they do so in different ways, they vibrate with a peaceful and positive atmosphere.

What have been the most surprising or unexpected things you've discovered about Bhutan?

Even though you don't find any traffic lights and roundabouts between and in the cities, yet the traffic is well organized, and the driving is very pleasant and respectful. Another thing we really enjoyed seeing is that many people have an altar at home where they would pray and meditate every morning.

Can you share any interesting cultural customs or traditions you've observed during your visit?

Vanita loved the traditional ladies' clothing so much that she bought two sets of Kira to wear during her travels around the world. Dino also happily wore a male Gho on many occasions during his stay in Bhutan.

A moment that we will never forget is when we were dressed in these traditional clothes and learned how to meditate with the singing bowl. It was just an amazing moment, and we actually bought one set of singing bowl to bring the tradition home with us.

What's the best way to connect with locals and immerse yourself in the culture here?

The best way to immerse yourself in the Bhutanese culture is by attending ceremonies and engaging with the locals as we did at Memorial Chorten in Thimphu and also at Gangtey Monastery.

We participated in making and lighting butter lamps followed by a prayer ceremony where many locals were chanting.

Connecting and building a friendship with our guide, Ugyen, was also a precious opportunity for us to understand more about the Bhutanese culture.

We had the chance to witness how families gather for a typical lunchtime together, and we are very grateful for this experience.

An international photographer, Dino Serrao, and his life and work partner, content creator Vanita Safaniuk, have led various projects in several countries, capturing the extraordinary within the ordinary. They have been featured on FOX USA and NRK (Norwegian TV). Today, Dino serves as an ambassador for Sony and, together with Vanita on their platforms, showcases the beauty of locals and the diversity yet uniqueness of humanity. Vanita also discusses cultures and places on her channels. It's a perfect combination of people and places! You can find them on Instagram at @dino.serrao and @vanitaiuk.

We enjoyed visiting the different attractions in Bhutan and capturing the beauty of the place and people

Is there a particular moment or experience from your trip that stands out as unforgettable?

The whole trip was unforgettable! Every encounter, and every moment shared with our guides and the locals.

The challenging uphill hike to the temple Baeyul Langdra and the effort we put in to reach this sacred place, followed by the privilege and immense pleasure of meeting MeyMey Pema and sharing a meditation with such an elevated soul, truly filled our souls. He also graciously allowed us to capture a portrait of him.

Any other thoughts/comments?

We can't wait to go back to Bhutan! We are so ready to have a new adventure in Bhutan again soon!

What are the differences between Bhutan and all the other destinations you've visited?

The simplicity of the people, their happiness, and the fact that they are not attached to materialism truly surprised us. We were amazed by how important spirituality is in their lives and how well we connected with the locals. We loved the purity of the country, its untouched beauty, and the locals' deep respect for nature and temples.

What is your impression of Bhutan before and after your trip?

Before going to Bhutan, we were told that Bhutan could be considered the Switzerland of Asia, but what we found out is that it is more than that!

We firmly believe that Bhutan is a pure and magical place. Even though it is a natural, simple country without big cities, it can offer so much to the world as an example of good living.

Lighting of butter lamps is a deeply spiritual practice in Bhutan

Grateful to have met Meymey Pema and shared a meditation session with him

The vibrations from the singing bowl positively affect one's mind and body

James Low

"The inner soul of Bhutan remains deep, strong, determined, and profoundly wise."

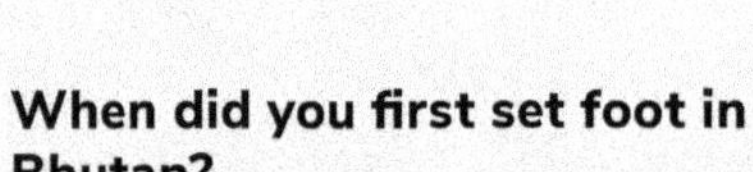

When did you first set foot in Bhutan?

I first arrived in Paro back in May 2004 to assist in the opening of COMO Uma Paro. At that time, I was the opening GM of COMO Metropolitan Bangkok and came up to assist in our sister property's opening. I made a few trips to Paro and then stayed in Bangkok for 11 years before transferring to Phuket to open the COMO Point Yamu. I stayed there for 3 and a half years and was assigned to COMO Uma Bhutan in October 2015. I have been here for 8 years now.

What are some qualities or traits that you admire about the Bhutanese?

The Bhutanese are very well known for their friendliness, sincerity, and good heartedness (kindness). They're proud of their heritage, and to a certain extent, selflessness.

What was your first impression of the country?

Back in 2004, I was too busy with the property's opening and did not venture out much in the Kingdom. I felt the isolation and untouched beauty of the country, a departure from what I was used to: an abundance of food choices, entertainment, shopping, and other material things that I was accustomed to in Thailand and Malaysia.

What are some of your most memorable experiences in Bhutan?

Sharing special moments with reincarnated monks and engaging in meaningful discussions with enlightened individuals who have stopped "chasing rainbows" to find contentment and inner peace.

Which is your favourite place in Bhutan?

That really depends on what I am looking for! When it comes to food, I have my go-to spots like Uma, San Maru for Korean, Druk Thimphu for Indian cuisine, and Hayate for ramen!

Other places I frequent are markets; Kaja Trom, the CSI market, Ogop, and Chuniding are some. For general sightseeing, my favorites are Chelela Pass (Prayer flags), Tiger's Nest, and Drakapor. The waterfall picnics (on the way to Gasa) are also a must-visit!

I also like off-beat monasteries like Gorina, Gangtey and Gasa.

In your opinion, how can travellers contribute to sustainable tourism in Bhutan?

Be responsible for your 'footprint' when you visit places in the Kingdom. It's the simple things like bringing a reusable water flask (never buying one-time plastic water bottles and food containers for picnics). Also, clean up after yourselves by bringing along trash bags when going out on treks.

Bring your own shopping totes for shopping and refuse plastic bags when offered. It's also encouraged to support charitable organizations when buying handicrafts, such as Renew, Desung, and OGOP. Support the cause, not just the message!

A portrait taken in COMO Uma Paro

What advice do you have for people who are contemplating to travel to Bhutan?

Find out what spurred your interest in visiting Bhutan. Was it a visual holiday? A quest for cultural knowledge? Outdoor pursuits like trekking, exploring flora and fauna, bird watching, or naturalist interests? Or perhaps it was for spirituality and self-discovery? Whatever your purpose, discuss these interests with your travel agent to plan a bespoke itinerary for you. Choose an appropriate travel season that aligns with your interests and itinerary.

The Land of the Thunder Dragon beckons and calls you to visit the Kingdom! Individuals themselves are never in control when making the decision to visit this very special Kingdom. When you are not ready, you will not find sufficient determination to be here. Come to Bhutan with an open mind and an open heart, and the Land will reward you with not just another holiday but a Journey of the Soul.

How has Bhutan changed your life?

Bhutan has this amazing energy of goodness that has been cocooned over generations upon generations from the rest of the world and somehow will reach out to your soul when you are ready to receive it.

When I took on this posting in Bhutan, I told the company I would only wish to be here for a maximum of two years as I was sure that I would feel restless, isolated (especially from my family residing in Malaysia). But after 3 months of landing in Bhutan, my mind opened up and so did my heart.

I started to look inwards, asking questions about my purpose in life, my own happiness, realization of gratitude, what true fulfillment felt like. It truly has opened up so many layers of self-realizations that I would never have unfolded in the outside world. I have stopped chasing rainbows now because I realized that I have found my golden pond in Bhutan.

The exterior of the luxurious COMO Uma Paro property

How do you think the country has changed over the decade? How would you describe Bhutan now compared to the early days of your visit?

I would say that Bhutan has evolved rather than changed. Perhaps the changes are superficial transformations that are more noticeable on the outer shell of the Kingdom, such as the capital city Thimphu and Paro, which have become much more developed and sophisticated, offering more choices in terms of food, shopping, and entertainment, with improved communication and connectivity to other parts of the Kingdom.

However, the inner soul of Bhutan remains deep, strong, determined, and profoundly wise. Its ageless patina and beauty are reflected in its culture, heritage, kindness, and spirituality.

Surprisingly, I have also matured in my outlook on life. I have come to appreciate what my part of the world lacks in comparison to Bhutan, such as its peacefulness, calmness, stunning mountain landscapes, pure fresh air, simplicity of life based on human values, and the desire to share kindness.

What are your hopes and aspirations for Bhutan?

My hope is that the goodness and energy of the Land will forever find solutions and will forever guide the Kingdom and her people to perpetual happiness.

James Low, a 45-year hotel industry veteran, has worked with renowned brands like Regent International, Holiday Inns Asia, Hyatt International, and Mandarin Oriental before joining COMO Hotels & Resorts. His journey with COMO Uma Bhutan began 19 years ago, and he later returned to oversee properties in Paro and Punakha. In Bhutan, he discovered a deep sense of belonging and became an ambassador for the country.

Bhutan's unique positive energy and culture deeply impacted James. Initially planning a short stay, he found inner growth and self-realization in Bhutan. He now manages COMO Resorts and mentors aspiring Bhutanese hotel professionals. His journey, spanning various countries, is a source of gratitude and a valuable experience he wishes to share with Bhutanese talents.

The traditional Bhutanese hot stone bath in COMO Uma Paro

Françoise Pommaret

"Forget about your preconceived ideas. Bhutan is different from any other country and does not conform to clichés."

When and how were you first introduced to Bhutan?

I first heard about Bhutan while studying Himalayan Culture at a university in France. I later visited as a guide for a French group in 1979. In 1981, I had the opportunity to return as a guest, and somehow, I am still here!

What was your first impression of the country?

At that time, we had to travel from India by road, so Bhutan was incredibly quiet, peaceful, and rural. It was also incredibly green, and the people were very hospitable.

What's the best way to connect with locals and immerse yourself in the culture here?

Visiting small local restaurants, stepping out of one's comfort zone, strolling through villages, and attending local festivals to mingle with the crowd and appreciate the deep-rooted faith of the Bhutanese.

How do you think the country has changed over the decades?

The changes are incredible. From an isolated country with hardly any communications, where there were only very small towns and few shops with the bare minimum, Bhutan has moved towards a more urban life. There are now many consumer products, good interconnections with the outside world, and digital communications. Roads, education, and health services have tremendously improved. People are generally much more prosperous, even though the human-wildlife conflict and climate change still make rural life challenging, leading to rural-urban migration.

How would you describe your experience living in Bhutan?

It is a story of resilience, friendship, and mutual assistance in a country that still preserves harmony between the physical and cultural landscape and its people. Living in Bhutan today involves a constant balance between cultural beliefs, traditions and the globalized world.

Taking a break while trekking in north eastern Bhutan

Field work with colleagues from the university

What are some of your most memorable experiences or encounters in Bhutan?

Every day is a memorable experience in Bhutan, but I would say interactions with people from all walks of life are among the best experiences. The feeling of security and tranquility are truly hallmarks of Bhutan. And, of course, the incredible ecological diversity of the country, ranging from semi-tropical jungles to eternal snows on such a small area of land, is remarkable.

Which is your favourite place in Bhutan?

Each place in Bhutan has its beauty and charm, and it all depends on what one is looking for or how one connects with the place. So it would not be fair for me to favor one particular place.

With the famous film director Pawo Choyning Dorji taken in December 2022

In Bhutanese traditional clothes, Kira

Françoise Pommaret (PhD), a scholar from the CNRS in France, has travelled all over the Himalayas and settled in Bhutan 40 years ago. She worked in the tourism, cultural heritage and higher education sectors trekking all over the country. She has produced several books and many articles on various aspects of Bhutanese culture. Honored with the French Legion of honour and the King's Gold medal, she is still passionate about Bhutan and currently serves as the French Honorary Consul in Bhutan.

Can you highlight some key distinctions between Bhutan and your country of origin?

Of course, France is very different from Bhutan, but there are many similarities: respect for cultural heritage, bawdy humor, attachment to the land, and a taste for good food.

What are some travel tips or advice you would give to someone planning a trip to Bhutan?

Forget about your preconceived ideas. Bhutan is different from any other country and does not conform to clichés. Come with an open mind and an open heart. Enjoy this incredible country!

What are some of your favourite food in Bhutan?

The "Bhutanese pizza", called menge, is made of rice with herb toppings, buckwheat noodles, pork cooked with chilies and turnips, and eggs with cheese.

What are your hopes and aspirations for Bhutan?

I just wish for the country to develop in a way that allows people to have a comfortable life while upholding their traditions. May it remain sovereign and peaceful!

Kristine Li

"The Bhutanese practise mindfulness the way it should be – It is what it is."

How were you first introduced to Bhutan?

I happened to come across a blogger (Yina Goh) who documented her trip to Bhutan!

How many times have you visited Bhutan

I've visited Bhutan three times and am looking forward to the next time I go back again! One of the trips was for a Neykor meditation retreat.

What were your most memorable experience for the Neykor meditation retreat?

We were at Burning Lake, with Khedrup Rinpoche guiding us through a meditation session by the lake. The weather was sunny but cold, and all of us were dressed in Bhutanese costumes.

The air smelled incredibly fresh, clean, and pure. During the peak of my meditation, there was a brief moment when my whole being felt overwhelmed with bliss, joy, and contentment, right then and there. That was the first time I experienced the healing power of meditation.

How did you find the Bhutanese people? Were there any interactions or encounters that stood out to you?

Bhutanese people mostly come across to me as gentle, shy, and wise individuals. This is evident in how they welcome foreign travelers; their hospitality made me feel like a guest in their country.

When we journeyed to the highlands of Merak, I was pleasantly surprised to find that, despite the nomadic highlanders living a life quite distinct from city-dwellers, I could interact with them in English. Furthermore, regardless of our location, be it the outskirts of eastern or central Bhutan or the mountains, the washrooms were consistently clean.

My hosts and guides from DrukAsia were easygoing individuals who always looked out for me during my trips. Their genuine warmth and concern continue to touch my heart when I recall those experiences.

What is the key difference between Bhutan and your country of origin?

Despite having a lot of material possessions, many of my Singaporean peers find it difficult to experience true happiness. In contrast, the Bhutanese, who do not have easy access to material goods, still find contentment and peace.

What aspect of Bhutanese culture do you find most admirable?

The Bhutanese people are what we would describe in Chinese as 內斂 (roughly translated to restrained/introverted/high level of self-control). This is one aspect of Bhutanese culture that I admire.

For some Bhutanese, their work environment and lives can be very challenging compared to the comforts of Western city culture – living in high mountains, dealing with harsh weather, and engaging in back-breaking work in rice fields or textile-weaving places. Yet, I have never seen a Bhutanese person who appeared bad-tempered from suppressing resentment about life and our endless material desires. They seem at peace! Achieving this level of contentment in life would require a high level of wisdom.

The Bhutanese practise mindfulness the way it should be – "It is what it is."

Additionally, it's always impressive how places are hardly messy or dirty, which reflects how the Bhutanese respect their environment.

A 5ft-petite travel blogger, yoga enthusiast, designer, and TCM wellness professional, Kristine Li, created The Petite Wanderess website – a travel & wellness blog – with a strong desire to showcase her collection of travel photos and provide essential travel tips for new destinations she explores.

In addition to curated travel images, Kristine shares stories of solo travel, her experiences hiking while petite and paranoid, integrating yoga and mindfulness into daily life, and the health benefits of practicing authentic Traditional Chinese Medicine.

As she navigates life's currents, Kristine finds herself drawn to natural places more than developed cities. Among the nearly 30 countries she has visited, her favorite destinations are Bhutan and Norway, which top her list.

Prayer flags are common sight throughout Bhutan

Which is your favourite place in Bhutan?

The hike to Tiger's Nest is one of my favorite experiences in Bhutan. Punakha Dzong is among the most beautiful places I've visited in Bhutan. I also appreciate the remoteness of Mongar district. Khedrup Rinpoche's monastery in central Bhutan, where we attended meditation workshops, has a field that overlooks the mountains. I enjoyed standing there and savoring the sunset views.

How has your spirituality evolved or grown as a result of your trip to Bhutan?

We are human beings here to learn many lessons in life, and when we break through with these learnings, that's when we can grow to become better people. Our conscious mind is superficial and relatively immature compared to our subconscious mind. Our eyes can also deceive us – what we see is often not the whole truth. We must rely on our inner wisdom to process and guide us.

Can you describe a moment during your trip that deeply touched you on a personal level?

When we were in Eastern Bhutan, we had finally arrived in Mongar after a long drive from Trashiyangtse. It was late afternoon when we stepped out of the hotel to explore the neighborhood.

In the distance, beyond the mountains, I could hear the soothing sound of prayer bells. The locals were leisurely enjoying the outdoor swings and facilities. The atmosphere felt incredibly relaxed, making me ponder that this is what life should be like. There's time for work, time for play, and time for relaxation. Life shouldn't always be rushed through.

What are some travel tips or advice you would give to someone planning a trip to Bhutan?

Go with an open mind!
The other tips are all on my article (https://thepetitewanderess.com/bhutan-trip-questions/). I love Bhutan and would like to send out all my well wishes to Bhutan!

At Sangchen Ogyen Tsuklag Monastery located in Trongsa, managed by Khedrupchen Rinpoche

Khedrupchen Rinpoche guiding us through a meditation session at the Burning Lake

Hiking up the Tiger's Nest with my lovely fellow Neykor retreat members

Walter Escaño

"It's like being transported to a magical place where you can immerse yourself in spirituality."

How many times have you visited Bhutan?

I have visited Bhutan twice. The first time was when the kingdom reopened during the pandemic in October 2022, and the second time was six months later in April 2023.

Fun Fact: On the second day of my first visit, I felt the magic of Bhutan and tried to extend my trip for a couple of days. However, flights back to Singapore were only available once a week back then, and I couldn't stay that much longer. At that moment, I knew I was going to visit again.

Did you travel solo or with a group?

I travelled solo on my first trip and then brought along 2 friends on my second trip.

What have been the most surprising or unexpected things you've discovered during your visit?

The spirituality of the kingdom and its people was palpable everywhere I went. It was humbling to witness how the teachings of Buddhism are applied in the daily lives of the Bhutanese people.

I heard many heartwarming stories about how the King helped the Bhutanese people during the pandemic, travelling around the country to personally check on them and using his personal resources to assist them. Their love for their King is overwhelming.

How would you describe Bhutan to your friends and family?

It's like being transported to a magical place where you can immerse yourself in spirituality, listen to your inner self, and move at your own pace. Savour each moment.

Why did you choose Bhutan as your travel destination?

Bhutan has always made headlines by measuring Gross National Happiness instead of the usual Gross Domestic Product used by other countries. This sparked my curiosity, leading me to spend a considerable amount of time reading numerous online articles and watching videos about the country.

As my knowledge about the country increased, my desire to visit and experience it in person grew stronger. I wanted to talk to the people, marvel at its pristine nature, appreciate its ancient and well-preserved architecture, savour the food, and explore a place that only a handful of people have been fortunate enough to visit.

A Filipino living in Singapore, Walter considers himself a lifelong learner. Having studied various fields such as Engineering, Accountancy, and Technology, he believes that exploring different places and getting to know people are two of life's best teachers. He enjoys taking family and friends on his travels and also relishes solo expeditions. Recently, he started learning video editing, which has become a means to share his travel experiences with the world through his Instagram and YouTube channel, @Walteroid.

Admiring the breathtaking Himalayan range

Chatting with the young nuns in Bhutan

What are some experiences from your trip that stands out as unforgettable?

There were many unforgettable moments during my trips to Bhutan, and below are some of them:

On my first trip to Bhutan, I was fortunate to be seated beside a kind Bhutanese gentleman, Mr. Sonam Tenzin. He patiently answered all of my questions about Bhutan and provided even more information about the country. After immigration, to my surprise, he waited and accompanied me in retrieving my luggage, exchanging money, and buying a SIM card. He didn't leave me until I was with my tour guide. This experience showcased how warm, welcoming, and thoughtful the Bhutanese people are.

As a fun fact, on my second trip to Bhutan, my friends and I met with him again. He and his friend, another Mr. Sonam, took us to dinner at a local restaurant and showed us the nightlife in Thimphu.

After completing my first trek to Tiger's Nest, back at the parking lot, I felt an indescribable burst of positive emotions. It was so overwhelming that I had to capture the moment on video. I wanted everyone to experience the same feeling that enveloped me at that time.

I had the opportunity to witness part of the last oral transmission led by the current Chief Abbot at Buddha Point, which involves the verbal passing of teachings from mouth to ear. It was a peaceful and solemn experience, and I got goosebumps seeing the Chief Abbot in person, walking only a few meters away from me. As I descended the stairs, I suddenly turned around and saw Buddha's head in the middle, surrounded by a sea of monks in their maroon robes descending the stairs on each side. It was mesmerising to watch, like angels descending from the heavens.

When I hiked uphill towards Dra Karpo to witness the pilgrims circumambulate the holy site 108 times, I was deeply touched by the selfless act of my tour guide. He carried a crate of water to give to the pilgrims. Upon reaching the top, two pilgrims who had been there for over 2 weeks approached him for mobile credits (load) so they could call their families back home, and he willingly provided it to them.

How did your interactions with the Bhutanese influence your own outlook on life?

The Bhutanese people, guided by the teachings of Buddhism (dharma), helped me progress in my journey of letting go of things I cannot control.

They taught me that living an austere life can lead to abundance in the things that truly matter, such as peace of mind, serenity, mental well-being, and good health.

Conversations with the nuns made me even more grateful for all the blessings in my life, no matter how big or small they may be.

A photo with the iconic Tiger's Nest monastery

Can you share any interesting cultural customs or traditions you've observed during your visit?

Paro Tsechu – It was a delight to see the Bhutanese people dressed in their finest Ghos and Kiras, having a marvelous time with their family and friends while watching the festival. The performers were adorned in colorful and intricately designed costumes, performing dances that incorporated graceful movements to express different stories and meanings.

I love how the Bhutanese wear their Ghos and Kiras with pride and a deep sense of nationalism. I wore the Gho a few times, and I felt smart and dignified. It was also interestingly the world's largest pocket!

Turning prayer wheels and circumambulating clockwise around a stupa or religious structure is a way to gain spiritual merit or blessings.

What advice would you give to individuals considering a trip to Bhutan?

Book that trip now! Keep an open and curious mind, embrace the culture and heritage, and engage with the warm people of Bhutan.

Linda Leaming

"This is a very beautiful and very quirky
place. In short, heaven."

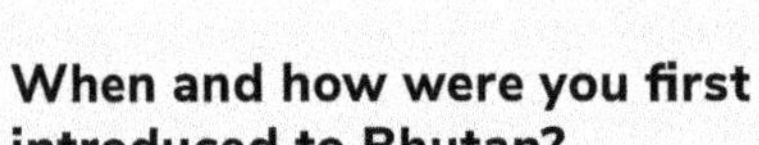

When and how were you first introduced to Bhutan?

I met some Bhutanese who were working at the UN in New York in the early 1990s. They were so easygoing, liked to joke around, and we used to have four-hour lunches in the middle of Manhattan. Who has four-hour lunches in Midtown Manhattan? Bhutanese, of course. My people.

How do you think the country has changed over the decades?

Thimphu has gotten bigger and faster with more cars and buildings. When I first came, there were 10,000 cars and about 30,000 people in Thimphu. Now, there are 127,000 cars and approximately 150,000 people. More Bhutanese are traveling, and there's a significant migration to Australia and Canada for education and work. However, some things have remained unchanged. Bhutan is still one of the most peaceful places on Earth. I pray it stays that way.

What are some of your most memorable experiences in Bhutan?

Getting married to a Bhutanese thanka painter. Adopting a little girl who had an aversion to school and speaking English. Building a house in an apple orchard above Thimphu. Living among people I love dearly in this extravagantly beautiful place.

What aspect of Bhutanese culture do you find most admirable?

The Bhutanese live their faith with positive results. They harbor no resentment towards anyone. They continue to instill good manners in their children. They have transformed this beautiful yet challenging land into something even more exceptional. They have a tendency to live in the moment.

What was your first impression of the country?

I first visited Bhutan in August 1994, coming from Delhi after a month of traveling in India. The plane ride offered breathtaking views of Mt. Everest and the Himalayas, and the aircraft itself seemed like a toy compared to the wide-bodied jets I had been on in India. The scale of things shifted even more dramatically when we arrived in Paro. The world felt lighter and easier. The scent of pine, followed by the tranquility and silence as we disembarked and made our way to the terminal, was incredibly soothing. Men in ghos and women in kira were all smiles. They looked genuinely happy to see us. I knew I was in a special place where magical things might happen, and I was right.

Mesmerising Tashichho Dzong illuminating the night

Linda Leaming was a harried American who traveled from Nashville, Tennessee, to Bhutan, first as a tourist and then to teach English and reconnect with a slower, happier way of life. She married Phurba Namgay, a Bhutanese artist, and learned to live more simply, slow down, and realize the unexpected path to happiness and accidental enlightenment.

She writes about her life in Bhutan and elsewhere in MARRIED TO BHUTAN: How One Woman Got Lost, Said 'I Do,' and Found Bliss (Hay House 2011, National Geographic 2012) and A FIELD GUIDE TO HAPPINESS: What I Learned in Bhutan About Living, Loving, and Waking Up (Hay House 2014). Her books have been translated into numerous languages.

Find her at www.marriedtobhutan.com and www.instagram.com/linda. leaming/

How would you describe your experience living in Bhutan?

Haha, it's kind of indescribable. I spend a lot of time pondering what it's like to live here. This place is exceptionally beautiful and delightfully quirky. In short, it's like heaven. Sometimes, as I walk around, I'm amazed at how closely we live in harmony with nature, which is quite unusual in this day and age. It's remarkably soothing, and with just a little effort and a few resources, one can make things better here.

Time feels different here, slower. It can be maddening at times, but mostly, it's charming. Living in Bhutan has been the most enriching ongoing experience of my life, and I'm grateful every day to be here.

In your opinion, how can travellers contribute to sustainable tourism in Bhutan?

I always encourage the travelers I meet to take a look at the amazing weaving in Bhutan and consider purchasing some if they're inclined. Bhutanese people are skilled weavers, creating some of the most beautiful and intricate weaving in the world. Bhutanese weaving is a living art, worn in daily life, and it's both distinctive and beautiful. Additionally, just by visiting, travelers contribute to the sustainability of Bhutan as the daily tariff of USD 100 supports hospitals, schools, and infrastructure.

Furthermore, if friends of Bhutan wish to further contribute to the well-being and sustainability of the country, they should check out www.bhutanfound.org, a brilliant organization that does important work in Bhutan.

With my Bhutanese husband, Phurba Namgay

Which is your favourite place in Bhutan?

I love the hike up to Cheri Monastery. It's about a 20-minute drive north of Thimphu to the beginning of the Jigme Dorji Wangchuck National Forest.

From there, you get out of the car and walk about 45 minutes up a path that switchbacks up the mountain. Stop and have a snack about three-quarters of the way up at the little chorten, painted white like the snow of Jumolhari. Be very quiet going up and down. Be mindful of where you place your feet and know that you are in an ancient place, a sacred place, where heaven and earth meet.

It was built by Shabdrung Ngawang Namgyal, the high holy man and unifier of Bhutan in the 17th century, as a meditation and retreat center, and it will become obvious to you why when you make the trip up. There's a palpable sense of calm there – calm within calm. But there's also a steady, vibrant energy. The view is, of course, spectacular. There are lovely temple rooms in the complex that you can visit, and once again, be very quiet and show reverence for the existence of such a place.

What are some travel tips or advice you would give to someone planning a trip to Bhutan?

Come and stay for as long as you can. Explore as deeply into the country as your time allows. Make Bhutan your primary destination. Instead of attempting to see half of Asia in two weeks, I suggest that, at least for a part of your time in Bhutan, you find a place, whether it's a cafe or a vegetable market, and sit down to enjoy a cup of tea or coffee while simply observing.

What are your hopes and aspirations for Bhutan?

I hope that Bhutan will thrive. I hope that Bhutan will remain safe. It's somewhat of a miracle that a place like Bhutan exists in the world, a combination of luck and good leadership. I hope that both the luck and the good leadership continue.

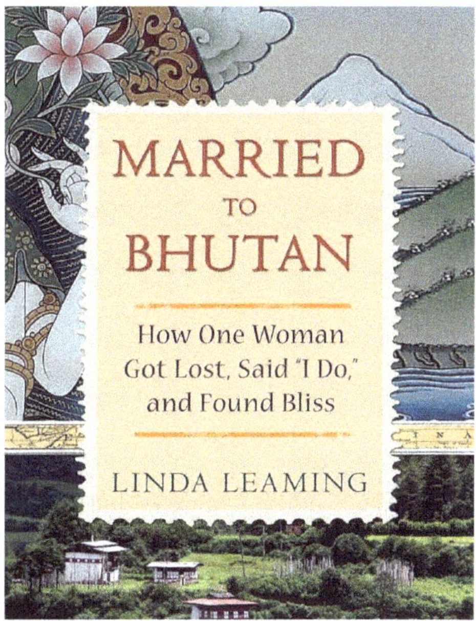

Married to Bhutan by Linda Leaming

Bradley Mayhew

"There is really nowhere on earth like Bhutan – nowhere that seems so immune to homogenous globalisation and commercialisation."

When and how were you first introduced to Bhutan?

I first came to Bhutan in 2010 while researching the fourth edition of the Lonely Planet guide to Bhutan. I had always wanted to visit the kingdom, after several trips to Tibet, Ladakh, Mustang, Dolpo, and Sikkim, but it was work that finally allowed me to get there. I was very excited to finally get on the plane to Paro.

How many times have you travelled to Bhutan?

Five trips so far, each about two months long, covering almost every part of the country from east to west, including some mountain trekking and all three overland crossings. I've been very lucky to have the time for such relatively long trips.

Which is your favourite hiking route in Bhutan? Why?

There are dozens of lovely hikes in Bhutan, particularly in areas like Haa, the Dochu La pass, and the valleys of Bumthang. It's worth considering a short hike along the long-distance Trans Bhutan Trail. The western section starting from the Dochu La pass leads you to one of Bhutan's two main craft beer breweries, which is a great way to quench your thirst after a walk.

What did you learn about Bhutan's history and heritage during your visit?

I learn a little more each time, as there are many layers to peel back in Bhutanese history, and there's only so much you can read in the limited literature. My first visit was focused on learning about traditional life and festivals. Subsequent visits have taught me more about the different religious lineages, how Bhutan fits into the Tibetan religious world, and how the religious and political aspects have often sat uncomfortably together throughout Bhutanese history. There's so much to learn!

What have been the most surprising or unexpected things you've discovered about Bhutan?

Every monastery or sacred spot has its own magical, surreal relics that push the boundaries of rational thought. I've seen stupas entombed in other stupas to stop them from flying away, religious paintings created from the nose blood of a saint, and even the mummified hand of a thief hanging in a protector chapel as a warning to other thieves. There's a magical and miraculous dimension to almost all temples in Bhutan.

Can you share any heartwarming or memorable encounters with the locals?

A couple of years ago, I posted a photo on Instagram of a young Bhutanese girl from Bumthang playing with her cute puppy. A week later, I received a comment from someone who thought it was her. It turned out to be her, and she was now a teenager living with her family in the USA. The rapid transformation that this young girl underwent, transitioning from traditional life in rural Bhutan to attending prom with a boyfriend in California, was truly remarkable to me. It was heartwarming to hear from her.

How is Bhutan different from all the other countries that you have visited?

The prioritisation of culture, tradition, and religion over immediate economic gain is the most significant distinction, and this is evident in the traditional architecture, attire, and the pristine forests. All of these elements have a profound visual impact on how you perceive the country.

What's your biggest takeaway from your trip to Bhutan?

There is really nowhere on earth like Bhutan – nowhere that seems so immune to homogenous globalisation and commercialisation. It's not perfect, but there is much to be learned from it.

Bradley Mayhew has been writing travel guidebooks for Lonely Planet for over 25 years now, covering destinations such as Tibet, Nepal, Trekking in the Nepal Himalaya, India, Central Asia, and the Silk Road. He has served as the primary author for five editions of Lonely Planet's Bhutan guide, including the most recent edition published in late 2023. Follow him on Instagram: @bradley_mayhew.

What's the best way to connect with locals and immerse yourself in the culture here?

Festivals are a great way to connect with locals on their terms. Sit with them in the crowd rather than in a foreigner-only VIP area, and you'll experience something quite different. Joining pilgrims on a hike to one of the country's many 'ney,' or sacred sites, is another excellent way to immerse yourself in local culture.

Local restaurants and bars in Thimphu provide a welcoming environment to engage with knowledgeable locals. Bhutanese people are very friendly and approachable.

Did you meet any locals or fellow travellers whose stories or wisdom had a profound impact on your personal growth?

Almost all the Bhutanese I met were inspiring examples of how to retain the perspective, grace, and wisdom of Buddhist teachings while embracing the modern world and technology.

Most Bhutanese I encountered had a profound respect for the environment and were willing to prioritise ethical action over financial gain, which I found quite inspiring. Few foreigners are ready to do that, even if they consider it wise in theory.

What advice do you have for travellers to Bhutan?

My best pieces of travel advice are as follows:

1) Don't try to cram too much into your itinerary; include some hikes, savour local meals, and allow time for independent exploration.

2) Visiting Bhutan can be expensive, but since you'll likely only visit once, consider adding a couple of extra days to your trip. You may not remember the cost in a year or two, but you will remember the additional places you explored and the extra time you had to fully immerse yourself.

In the Bhutanese traditional male attire, Gho

Witnessing the unfurling of thangka during Bhutanese festival at Chorten Kora

Traversing the breathtaking trails of Bhutan with Druk Asia in 2023

Write a review of Bhutan Travelog

If you've enjoyed reading the book, we'd be truly grateful if you could share your thoughts by leaving a review on **www.bhutantravelog.com.**

Bonus

As a little treat, check out the link below for some lovely ongoing promotions to help you save on your next Bhutan adventure.

facebook.com/bhutantravelog

@bhutantravelog

@bhutantravelog

Check out **www.bhutantravelog.com** for more Bhutan travel inspirations.

Bhutan in a Nutshell

1. One of the safest countries in the world

Bhutan has effectively handled the COVID-19 pandemic. With just 37 doctors, 1,200 vaccination centres and less than 3,000 healthcare workers, 95% of its eligible population are fully vaccinated, as of July 2021.

2. Top sustainable green destination

Green Destinations awarded Bhutan with the Earth Award in 2018 and Gold Award in 2019 for its sustainable and green initiatives, topping 100 sustainable destinations in the world.

3. Birthplace of Gross National Happiness (GNH)

Upon Bhutan's proposal, the United Nations has adopted happiness as a development indicator. Since 2012, March 20 is celebrated as International Happiness Day.

4. A country that doesn't have any traffic lights

You will not find a single traffic light in the entire country. Instead, you'll see traffic police controlling the traffic in the heart of the capital city, Thimphu.

5. 'High value, Low volume' sustainable tourism policy

Unlike other destinations, you will not suffer from overcrowding at tourist attractions. In fact, places are so quiet, you can take your time with a proper photoshoot.

6. The only carbon negative country in the world

Today, Bhutan is the only carbon negative country in the world. It's no surprise that some say there's magic in the air.

7. Home to the highest unclimbed mountain in the world

Since Bhutan prohibits mountaineering beyond 6,000 metres, Gangkar Puensum, standing at 7,570 metres above sea level, is the world's highest unclimbed mountain.

8. Locals live in harmony with nature

The Bhutanese have the utmost respect for the natural environment including the forests, rocks, cliffs, lakes, rivers, water springs and mountains. They are deemed abodes of the local deities.

9. Bhutan is one of the most peaceful places in the world

The Bhutanese take great pride living in Bhutan, a very peaceful and safe country. There are few crimes reported in the country, including in the major districts.

10. Democracy in Bhutan is a gift from the throne

"We cannot leave such a small, vulnerable country in the hands of one person, who is chosen by birth and not by merit. Therefore, the Bhutanese must choose their own leader," said the fourth King, Jigme Singye Wangchuck.

11. A country blessed with compassionate and visionary monarchs

The Bhutanese have a deep love and respect for their king. The kings of Bhutan have always put the country before themselves. As such, the monarchs have constantly been a source of inspiration to the Bhutanese.

12. One of the top biodiversity hotspots in the world

You can find thriving populations of endangered animals in Bhutan due to their efforts in protection and conservation. Currently, there are five national parks, four wildlife sanctuaries and one nature reserve that covers 51.32% of the country's area.

13. The most hospitable people that you'll ever meet

The Bhutanese are incredibly kind, generous and warm people. They'll not hesitate to offer their help. You can rest assured that your safety and wellbeing are taken care of when you're in the country. Also, Bhutanese have common names. So, don't be surprised if you meet plenty of new friends named Ugyen, Sonam, Karma, Kinley or Pema.

14. Strong cultural identity and traditions

Bhutan is a country rich in cultural heritage. It has a lot to offer to travellers from abroad. The fabled kingdom boasts centuries-old architecture, sacred dances, significant Buddhist rituals, and highly devoted people.

15. Spectacular landscapes that are feasts for the eyes

The kingdom has an unspoiled natural environment, an extensive range of flora and fauna, spectacular Himalayan mountains, and an atmosphere that makes you want to visit again and again.

16. Healthy diet and lifestyle

If you're a health-conscious person, you can get relief knowing that Bhutanese food is healthy as most ingredients are grown organically within the country. In fact, the kingdom has an audacious goal to become the first wholly organic nation.

17. A very accessible tourist destination

Bhutan is definitely a remote country that's easily accessible if you want to travel off the beaten track to explore somewhere exclusive. There are direct flights from various Asian countries such as Bangkok, Singapore, India, Bangladesh and Nepal.

18. Bhutan is a country that will enrich you spiritually

In Bhutan, everything has a story, a meaning, or a lesson. Many people travel to Bhutan to seek inner peace and escape from the hustle and bustle of city life. It's the perfect location to contemplate the deeper meanings of life. But, one can only feel its true essence and magic by being physically there to experience it.

Glossary

Ara
Rice wine.

Atsara
Jesters or clowns who entertain the crowd during a tshechu.

Bangchu
Circular bamboo container with a lid.

Bodhisattva
Enlightened beings in Mahayana Buddhism.

Bon
Religion with shamanistic and animist practices that predate Buddhism in the Himalayan region.

Bonpo
Bon priests.

Brokpas
Inhabitants of the valleys of Merak and Sakteng in eastern Bhutan.

Bumpa
Sacred vessel.

Bukhari
Traditional wood-burning stove.

Chhu
River or water.

Choesi
Dual system of governance.

Choesum
An elaborately decorated shrine room with an altar that also serves as a guest room.

Chorten
Religious structure, also known as stupa, usually containing sacred relics.

Chugo
A hard cheese made from yak's milk.

Dapa
Lustrous wooden bowl or cup.

Dasho
An honorary title conferred by the king.

Desi
Title given to the temporal ruler of Bhutan from 1851 to 1905.

Desuung
Guardians of Peace.

Doma
Areca nut and slaked lime wrapped in betel leaf.

Dorje
Thunderbolt.

Dratshang
Commision for the Monastic Affairs in Bhutan.

Driglam Namzha
Official code of etiquette and dress code in Bhutan.

Druk
Thunder Dragon.

Druk Gyalpo
Formal title held by the ruler of Bhutan, the King of Bhutan.

Drukpa
People from Bhutan.

Druk Yul
Land of the Thunder Dragon, the name for Bhutan in Dzongkha.

Drukpa Kargyupa
The sect of Buddhism that is the official state religion of Bhutan.

Drukpa Kuenley
Saint of the Drukpa Kagyu school, who spread his unorthodox teachings.

Duar
Doorway or gate, which refers to the
traditional entrances to Bhutan from the
Bengal and Assam plains of India.

Dungpa
Administrator of a sub-district.

Dzong
Ancient fortress in Bhutan that usually
houses administrative offices as well as the
monastic body.

Dzongda
Administrative head of a district.

Dzongkha
The official language of Bhutan (literally,
language spoken in the dzong).

Dzongkhag
District.

Ema datsi
Dish of chillies cooked with cheese.

Ezay
A chutney or relish made with chillies.

Gewog
A county consisting of a block of villages.

Gho
Men's traditional dress; a knee-length robe
secured with a handwoven belt.

Goen Hogay
Cucumber salad.

Goenkhang
Inner sanctum.

Gomchen
Lay monk or ascetic.

Gompa
Monastery.

Gyalsung
National service.

Guru Padmasambhava
The Indian saint who brought Buddhism to
Bhutan in the eighth century; also popularly
known as Guru Rinpoche.

Je Khenpo
Chief Abbot of Bhutan, and official head of the
Drukpa Kagyu school.

Jigme Dorji Wangchuck
Third King of Bhutan.

Jigme Khesar Namgyel Wangchuck
Fifth King of Bhutan.

Jigme Namgyel
Tongsa Penlop and fiftieth desi of Bhutan;
father of the first King.

Jigme Singye Wangchuck
Fourth King of Bhutan.

Jigme Wangchuck
Second King of Bhutan.

Kabney
Ceremonial scarf worn by men.

Karma
The universal law of cause and effect.

Kasho
Royal decree.

Kera
Woven belt.

Kewa datshi
Potato cheese.

Khuru
A game of darts.

Kira
Women's traditional dress, an ankle-length
dress held together by a brooch.

Koma
Brooches to fasten the women's *kira* at
the shoulder.

Kishuthara
An elaborate and intricately woven Bhutanese textile.

La
Mountain pass.

Lam Neten
Head abbot of a district.

Lama
Buddhist priest who is a religious master.

Layaps
People from Laya in the northern highlands of Bhutan.

Lhakhang
Buddhist temple.

Lhotsampa
Persons of Nepali origin who are settled in Bhutan.

Mani wall
Stone walls carved with the Buddhist mantra: Om mani padme hum.

Ney
Sacred site.

Ngultrum
Bhutanese currency (BTN).

Penlop
Historic title given to governors of the three big dzongs of Paro, Trongsa and Daga.

Rachu
Women's ceremonial scarf; draped over the left shoulder.

Rinpoche
The 'precious one'; reincarnated lama.

Sharchopkha
The language spoken in eastern Bhutan.

Songtsen Gampo
King of Tibet in the seventh century who built the first Buddhist temples in Bhutan.

Samsara
The continuous cycle of life, death and reincarnation.

Shamu Datshi
Mushroom cheese.

Stupa
A dome-shaped Buddhist shrine.

Suja
Butter tea.

Takin (Budorcas taxicolor)
National animal of Bhutan, scientifically classified as a goat-antelope, found in the highlands of Bhutan.

Terma
Hidden treasure.

Terton
Treasure revealer.

Thangka
Buddhist scroll painting.

Thongdrel
Large painted or embroidered silk banners hung from the wall of a dzong or monastery on important religious occasions.

Trulku
Reincarnated master; spiritual head of a monastery.

Tsatsa
Miniature cylindrical-shaped stupas made from clay and sometimes mixed with ashes of the deceased.

Tshachu
Hot spring.

Tsatsi Buram
Sweet made from sugarcane.

Tshechu
Religious festival held in honour of Guru Padmasambhava.

Tsho
Lake.

Tshogdu
National Assembly of Bhutan.

Ugyen Wangchuck
First King of Bhutan.

Utse
Central tower of a dzong.

Wonju
Women's long-sleeved blouse, worn under
the *kira*.

Yathra
Colourful woollen textile woven in the
Bumthang district of Bhutan.

Zaw
Roasted rice.

Zorig Chusum
The thirteen traditional arts and crafts of
Bhutan.

Ashley Chen

Ashley is an avid traveller with a deep curiosity for the world's diverse cultures and beliefs. Beyond her love for writing and photography, she is a reflective wanderer with a philosophical outlook, always seeking to understand more about herself and the world around her.

As the editor of *Daily Bhutan*—an independent publication sharing the latest news, educational features, and inspiring stories from Bhutan—Ashley is dedicated to amplifying Bhutan's voice on the global stage. She holds a profound admiration for Bhutan's heritage and deeply respects the pride that Bhutanese people carry for their nation.

When in Bhutan, Ashley blends effortlessly into the local rhythm of life, often mistaken for a native. She believes that every person carries a unique story and perspective, and she treasures meaningful conversations with those she meets along her journeys.

Joni Herison

Joni has been involved in Bhutan's tourism industry for more than a decade. It all started with his first trip to the Kingdom when he was introduced to the concept of "travelling right" in Bhutan – the importance of traveling on a private tour with a local guide so visitors can benefit from a deeper appreciation of the cultural, historical, and natural aspects of Bhutan.

This philosophy not only shaped his personal approach to travel but also influenced Joni to start Druk Asia, one of the pioneering Bhutan tour operators outside of Bhutan. As Managing Director of Druk Asia, Joni has played a pivotal role in connecting Bhutan with travellers from all over the world and is a cherished friend of the kingdom.

He has a deep love for the kingdom and has built an excellent rapport with the Bhutanese community. Joni has visited Bhutan 40 times since 2008. Each of his visits to the kingdom rejuvenated his spirits and spurred him to continue promoting Bhutan as a travel destination.

A bibliophile with a cheerful disposition, Joni can always be found with a cup of coffee and a book at hand. Indonesian by birth and Bhutanese by heart, Joni has put down roots in Singapore with his lovely wife, Eileen, and three adorable children.

Established in 2009, Druk Asia stands as a trailblazing tour operator with a profound passion for Bhutan. Over the past decade, we have thrived as a tight-knit team of 20 dedicated tour guides who share a deep affection for this enchanting land and a common mission: ensuring our customers' utmost satisfaction.

Our tour guides are not just professionals; they are beacons of sincerity, earnestness, and unrivalled knowledge, earning the admiration of all our cherished guests.

At Druk Asia, every tour we craft is a private and personalized adventure. Whether you're a solo explorer in search of a life-changing journey through Bhutan's mystical landscapes or part of a sizable group, our extensive experience allows us to cater to your unique needs, preferences, and interests.

Beyond conventional sightseeing, we offer a variety of special tours that infuse excitement into your Bhutan experience. Explore the world of guided-sketching tours, find inner peace through meditation tours, capture unforgettable memories with pre-wedding photoshoot tours, or sharpen your photography skills on our specialized photography tours. For corporate entities and social clubs, we also offer MICE services, ensuring memorable events against Bhutan's breathtaking backdrop.

Since 2012, we have proudly served as the official General Sales Agent for Royal Bhutan Airlines (Drukair). This enduring partnership symbolises our commitment to making Bhutan accessible to travelers from across the globe, sharing in the wonder and magic of this remarkable kingdom.

For more information or to get in touch with our travel specialists, check out
www.drukasia.com.

www.ingramcontent.com/pod-product-compliance
Lightning Source LLC
Chambersburg PA
CBHW061133160726
48006CB00037B/1990